GODOT FROM ZERO TO PROFICIENCY

(FOUNDATIONS)

First Edition

A step-by-step guide to creating your first 3D game environment in Godot.

Patrick Felicia

GODOT FROM ZERO TO PROFICIENCY

(FOUNDATIONS)

- First published: March 2021.
- Updated on December 2025

Published by Patrick Felicia

CREDITS

Author: Patrick Felicia

ABOUT THE AUTHOR

Patrick Felicia is a lecturer and researcher at Waterford Institute of Technology, where he teaches and supervises undergraduate and postgraduate students. He obtained his MSc in Multimedia Technology in 2003 and PhD in Computer Science in 2009 from University College Cork, Ireland. He has published several books and articles on the use of video games for educational purposes, including the Handbook of Research on Improving Learning and Motivation through Educational Games: Multidisciplinary Approaches (published by IGI), and Digital Games in Schools: a Handbook for Teachers, published by European Schoolnet. Patrick is also the Editor-in-chief of the International Journal of Game-Based Learning (IJGBL), and the Conference Director of the Irish Symposium on Game-Based Learning, a popular conference on games and learning organized throughout Ireland.

SUPPORT AND RESOURCES FOR THIS BOOK

To complete the activities presented in this book you need to download the startup pack on the companion website; it consists of free resources that you will need to complete your projects. To download these resources, do the following:

- Open the page **http://www.learntocreategames.com/books**.

- Click on your book (**Godot From Zero to Proficiency (Foundations)**)

Download your FREE

Resource Pack!

Please enter your name and email address below to receive your resource pack and complete the projects in your book. You will also receive regular updates and tutorials Games Programming and other Programming topics..

Name

Email

You can unsubscribe anytime. For more details, review our Privacy Policy.

- In the new page, click the link that says "**Download Your Resource Pack**"

This book is dedicated to Mathis

TABLE OF CONTENTS

Contents

PREFACE

This book will show you how you can very quickly start using Godot, a lightweight engine that makes it possible to create games.

Although it may not be as powerful as Unity or Unreal yet, it offers a wide range of features for you to create your own video games. More importantly, this game engine is both Open Source and lightweight which means that even if you have (or you are teaching with) computers with very low technical specification, you should still be able to use Godot, and teach or learn how to code while creating video games.

This book series entitled **Godot From Zero to Proficiency** gives you the opportunity to play around with Godot's core features, and essentially those that will make it possible to create interesting 3D and 2D games rapidly. After reading this book series, you should find it easier to use Godot and its core functionalities.

This book series assumes no prior knowledge on the part of the reader, and it will get you started on Godot so that you quickly master all the wonderful features that this software provides by going through an easy learning curve.

By completing each chapter, and by following step-by-step instructions, you will progressively improve your skills, become more proficient in Godot, and create a survival game using Godot's core features in terms of programming (i.e., GDScript), game design, and drag and drop features.

In addition to understanding and being able to master Godot's core features, you will also create a game that includes many of the common techniques found in video games, including level design, object creation, textures, collision detection, lights, weapon creation, character animations, particles, artificial intelligence, and menus.

Throughout this book series, you will create a game that includes both indoor and outdoor environments where the player needs to find his/her way out of the former through tunnels, escalators, traps, and other challenges, avoid or eliminate enemies using weapons (i.e., gun or grenades), and drive a car or pilot an aircraft.

You will learn how to create customized menus and simple user interfaces using Godot's UI system and animate and give (artificial) intelligence to Non-Player Characters (NPCs) that will be able to follow your character using path finding.

Finally, you will also get to export your game at the different stages of the books, so that you can share it with your friends and obtain some feedback as well.

CONTENT COVERED BY THIS BOOK

Chapter 1, *The Benefits of Using Godot*, provides general information on game engines and explains why you should use such software, and how, by using Godot more specifically, you can create games seamlessly.

Chapter 2, *Installing Godot and Becoming Familiar with the Interface*, takes you through the very first steps of installing Godot and becoming familiar with the interface. It will also show you the different shortcuts necessary to navigate through scenes and projects in Godot.

Chapter 3, *Creating and Exporting your First Scene*, gets you to create and export your first scene by combining built-in objects. You will learn how to manage objects, apply textures and colors, and transform objects to create a simple scene.

Chapter 4, *Transforming Built-in Objects to Create an Indoor Scene*, explains how you can create an indoor scene (i.e., a maze) with built-in shapes. You will also work with and manage lights in your scene to set the atmosphere and navigate through the scene with a First-Person Controller.

Chapter 5, *Creating an outdoor Scene with Godot's Built-in Terrain Generator*, explains how you can create an outdoor scene with water, hills, sandy beaches, and palm trees using Godot's built-in assets.

Chapter 6 provides answers to frequently asked questions based on specific themes and topics (e.g., asset creation or transformations).

Chapter 7 summarizes the topics covered in this book and also provides useful information if you would like to progress further with this book series.

WHAT YOU NEED TO USE THIS BOOK

To complete the project presented in this book, you only need **Godot 4** (or a more recent version), and to also ensure that your computer and its operating system comply with Godot's requirements. Godot can be downloaded from the official website (http://www.godotengine.org/download), and before downloading, you can check that your computer fulfills the requirements for Godot on the same page.

At the time of writing this book, the following operating systems are supported by Godot for development: Windows, Linux and Mac OS X.

In terms of computer skills, all knowledge introduced in this book will assume no prior programming experience from the reader. This book does not include any programming, as this will be introduced in the second book in the series. So, for now, you only need to be able to perform common computer tasks such as downloading files, opening and saving files, be comfortable with dragging and dropping items, and typing.

WHO THIS BOOK IS FOR

If you can answer **yes** to all these questions, then this book is for you:

1. Are you a total beginner in Godot?

2. Would you like to become proficient in the core functionalities offered by Godot?

3. Would you like to teach students or help your child to understand how to create games?

4. Would you like to start creating great 3D games?

5. Although you may have had some prior exposure to Godot, would you like to delve more into Godot and understand its core functionalities in more detail?

WHO THIS BOOK IS NOT FOR

If you can answer yes to all these questions, then this book is **not** for you:

1. Can you already easily create a 3D game with Godot with built-in objects, controllers, cameras, lights, and terrains?

2. Are you looking for a reference book on Godot programming?

3. Are you an experienced (or at least advanced) Godot user?

If you can answer yes to all three questions, you may instead look for the next books in the series. To see the content and topics covered by these books, you can check the official website (**www.learntocreategames.com/books/**).

HOW YOU WILL LEARN FROM THIS BOOK

Because all students learn differently and have different expectations of a course, this book is designed to ensure that all readers find a learning mode that suits them. Therefore, it includes the following:

- A list of the learning objectives at the start of each chapter so that readers have a snapshot of the skills that will be covered.

- Each section includes an overview of the activities covered.

- Many of the activities are step-by-step, and learners are also given opportunities to engage in deeper learning and problem-solving skills through the challenges offered at the end of each chapter.

- Each chapter ends-up with a quiz and challenges through which you can put your skills into practice and see how much you know.

- The book focuses on the core skills that you need. Some sections also go into more detail. However, once the concepts have been explained, links are provided to additional resources, if and where necessary.

FORMAT OF EACH CHAPTER AND WRITING CONVENTIONS

Throughout this book, and to make reading and learning easier, text formatting and icons will be used to highlight parts of the information provided and to make it more readable.

SPECIAL NOTES

Each chapter includes resource sections so that you can further your understanding and mastery of Godot. These include:

- A quiz for each chapter: these quizzes usually include 10 questions that test your knowledge of the topics covered throughout the chapter. The solutions are provided on the companion website.

- A checklist: it consists of between 5 and 10 key concepts and skills that you need to be comfortable with before progressing to the next chapter.

- Challenges: each chapter includes a challenge section where you are asked to combine your skills to solve a particular problem.

The author's notes appear as described below:

> Author's suggestions appear in this box.

Checklists that include the important points covered in the chapter appear as described below:

- Item1 for check list

- Item2 for check list

- Item3 for check list

HOW CAN YOU LEARN BEST FROM THIS BOOK

- **Talk to your friends about what you are doing.**

  We often think that we understand a topic until we have to explain it to friends and answer their questions. By explaining your different projects, what you just learned will become clearer to you.

- **Do the exercises.**

  All chapters include exercises that will help you to learn by doing. In other words, by completing these exercises, you will be able to better understand the topic and you will gain practical skills (i.e., rather than just reading).

- **Don't be afraid of making mistakes.**

  I usually tell my students that making mistakes is part of the learning process. The more mistakes you make and the more opportunities you have for learning. At the start, you may find the errors disconcerting, or that the engine does not work as expected until you understand what went wrong.

- **Export your games early.**

  It is always great to build and export your first game. Even if it is rather simple, it is always good to see it in a browser and to be able to share it with you friends.

- **Learn in chunks.**

  It may be disconcerting to go through five or six chapters straight, as it may lower your motivation. Instead, give yourself enough time to learn, go at your own pace, and learn in small chunks (e.g., between 15 and 20 minutes per day). This will do at least two things for you: it will give your brain the time to "digest" the information that you have just learned, so that you can start fresh the following day. It will also make sure that you don't "burn-out" and that you keep your motivation levels high.

FEEDBACK

While I have done everything possible to produce a book of high quality and value, I always appreciate feedback from readers so that the book can be improved accordingly. If you would like to give feedback, you can email me at **learntocreategames@gmail.com**.

DOWNLOADING THE SOLUTIONS FOR THE BOOK

To complete the activities presented in this book you need to download the startup pack on the companion website; it consists of free resources that you will need to complete your projects. To download these resources, do the following:

- Open the page **http://www.learntocreategames.com/books**.

- Click on your book (**Godot From Zero to Proficiency (Foundations)**)

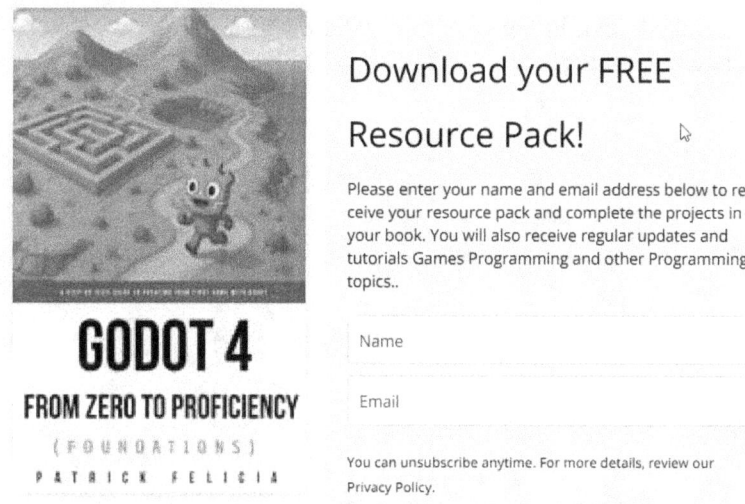

Download your FREE

Resource Pack!

Please enter your name and email address below to receive your resource pack and complete the projects in your book. You will also receive regular updates and tutorials Games Programming and other Programming topics..

Name

Email

You can unsubscribe anytime. For more details, review our Privacy Policy.

- In the new page, click the link that says "**Download Your Free Resource Pack**"

IMPROVING THE BOOK

Although great care was taken in checking the content of this book, I am human, and some errors could remain in the book. As a result, it would be great if you could let me know of any issue or error you may have come across in this book, so that it can be solved, and the book updated accordingly. To report an error, you can email me (**learntocreategames@gmail.com**) with the following information:

- Name of the book.

- The page where the error was detected.

- Describe the error and also what you think the correction should be.

Once your email is received, the error will be checked, and, in the case of a valid error, it will be corrected, and the book page will be updated to reflect the changes accordingly.

SUPPORTING THE AUTHOR

A lot of work has gone into this book, and it is the fruit of long hours of preparation, brainstorming, and finally writing. As a result, I would ask that you do not distribute any illegal copies of this book.

This means that if a friend wants a copy of this book, s/he will have to buy it through the official channels or the book's official website: **www.learntocreategames.com/books**.

If some of your friends are interested in the book, you can refer them to the book's official website (**http://www.learntocreategames.com/books**) where they can either buy the book, enter a monthly draw to be in for a chance of receiving a free copy of the book, or be notified of future promotional offers.

CHAPTER 1: THE BENEFITS OF USING GODOT

This chapter is an introduction to game engines and to Godot, and it explains the benefits brought by game engines, and more specifically how Godot can help you to create games seamlessly. The most recent features are explained, and examples of games created in Godot are also given so that you can evaluate the potential of this game engine.

If you already know of the benefits of Godot and game engines in general, you can skip this chapter.

After completing this section, you should be able to:

- Understand the concept of game engines.

- Know the features introduced by Godot 4.

- Understand the benefits of using Godot.

WHAT IS A GAME ENGINE AND SHOULD YOU USE ONE?

Godot makes it possible to create video games without knowing some of the underlying technologies of game development, so that potential game developers only need to focus on the game mechanics and employ a high-level approach to creating games using programming and scripting languages such as C# or Python. The term **high-level** here refers to the fact that when you create a game with a game engine, you don't need to worry about how the software will render the game or how it will communicate with the graphics card to optimize the speed of your game. So using a game engine would generally offer the following features and benefits:

- Accelerated development: game engines make it possible to focus on the game mechanics. Because built-in libraries are available for common mechanics and features, these do not need to be rebuilt from scratch, and programmers can use them immediately and save time (e.g., for the user interface or the artificial intelligence).

- Integrated Development Environment (IDE): an IDE helps to create, compile, and manage your code, and includes some useful tools that make development and debugging more efficient.

- Graphical User Interface (GUI): while some game engines are based on libraries, most common game engines make it possible for users to create objects seamlessly and to perform common tasks such as transforming, texturing, and animating assets, through drag and drop features. Another advantage of such software is that you can understand and preview how the game will look without having to compile the code beforehand (e.g., through scenes).

- Multi-platform deployment: with common game engines, it is possible to easily export the game that you have created to several platforms (e.g., for the web, iOS, or Android) without having to recode the entire game.

ADVANTAGES OF USING GODOT

There are several game engines available out there. However, Godot, which is a relatively recent game engine has proven to be a very good game engine, and more importantly, it is lightweight and very easy to install and use.

With Godot, you can create 2D or 3D games and produce several types of game genres including First-Person Shooters (FPS), Role Playing Games (RPG), casual games, adventure games, and much more.

In addition to being able to create a wide range of video games with an easy-to-use interface, Godot makes it possible to export games to a wide range of platforms, including mobile platforms including Android, iOS, Windows, MacOS or Linux.

Godot includes all the necessary tools that you need to create great games and it also simplifies the application of useful techniques to improve the quality of your game.

Finally, in order to control the game, you can use high-level programming and scripting languages such as C# or GDScript (similar to Python). This is useful for those who have already been exposed to similar languages to transfer their skills to game programming in Godot.

NOVELTIES INTRODUCED IN GODOT 1–4 (UPDATED FOR GODOT 4.5)

Godot is now in the **4.x** series (with Godot **4.5** at the time of writing). The engine has evolved rapidly since its first public release, with each major version introducing new tools, workflows, and performance improvements. The Godot team continues to develop the engine at an impressive pace, fixing issues quickly and refining the overall experience for developers.

While future versions will undoubtedly add new capabilities, **the foundations and core concepts you will learn in this book remain valid**, because Godot's design philosophy has stayed consistent across versions.

Here is a brief overview of Godot's evolution:

- **Godot 1 (2014)**
  The first public release. Already included many essential game-engine features such as lightmapping, shaders, animation tools, navigation, and a node-based scene system.

- **Godot 2 (2016)**
  Introduced major usability improvements, including **scene instancing**, **node inheritance**, an improved **debugger**, and refinements to the editor and workflow.

- **Godot 3 (2018)**
  A major step forward. Added **physically based rendering (PBR)**, a rewritten 3D engine, **C# support**, **visual scripting**, **VR/AR support**, and **WebAssembly exporting**. This version made Godot competitive for both 2D and 3D production.

- **Godot 4 (2023–present)**
  A complete redesign of large parts of the engine. Key improvements include:

  o A modernised **rendering engine** (Forward+ and Mobile renderers)

  o Better **lighting and shadows**

o   Significant improvements in **3D performance**

o   New **navigation and physics engines**

o   Overhauled **animation system**

o   A redesigned **GDScript**, faster and more expressive

o   Major updates to **2D tools**, TileMaps, and level editing

o   Ongoing refinement in Godot **4.1 → 4.5**, making the engine more stable and production-ready

As you can see, Godot has grown into a powerful, modern game engine suitable for both beginners and professionals. In this book series, we focus on **Godot's core technologies**, giving you a strong foundation that will remain relevant across all future 4.x updates.

LEVEL ROUNDUP

Summary

This chapter has described some of the reasons why you should use Godot and some of its core functionalities. You have also discovered the concept of game engines, the benefits brought by game engines, and how Godot can specifically make it easier for you to get started with game development.

CHAPTER 2: INSTALLING GODOT AND BECOMING FAMILIAR WITH THE INTERFACE

This chapter helps you to progressively become familiar with Godot by explaining and illustrating how to install this software, and how the different views and core features can be employed. You will also learn to create your first project and scene, using predefined objects such as boxes. After learning the features of the different views available in Godot, you will learn how to navigate through a scene (to look at objects), before creating your very first game environment with built-in objects and applying colors and textures.

After completing this section, you should be able to:

- Be more comfortable with Godot's interface.

- Understand the role and location of the different views in Godot.

- Understand the role of colliders.

- Add and configure cameras and lights.

- Know and use shortcuts to manipulate objects (e.g., move, scale, resize, duplicate, or delete) and move the view accordingly (e.g., pan or rotate).

- Create and apply colors and textures to objects.

- Create and combine simple built-in shapes.

- Know how to search for and organize assets in your game efficiently.

- Navigate through your scene.

DOWNLOADING GODOT

Now that you have had an overview of Godot and game engines, it is time for us to start using Godot. However, before you can install and use Godot, you will need to download and install *Godot* using the following steps:

1. open the following link: **https://godotengine.org/download/**.

2. A new page will automatically load depending on your operating system; for example, if you are using Mac OS, the page **https://godotengine.org/download/osx** will open, and if you are using Windows, the page **https://godotengine.org/download/windows** will open instead.

3. check the requirements for installing Godot on your computer listed on that page.

4. Once you have checked the requirements, we can start to download Godot: you will have the choice to download the **Standard Version** or the **Mono Version (C# support)**. Because we will be using GSScript in this book series, click on the link for the **Standard Version**.

5. After clicking on the button for the **Standard Version** of Godot, the download should start, and the application should be downloaded to your computer.

6. After a few seconds, depending on your connection speed, a zip file containing the application should have been downloaded.

7. You can then unzip this file and run Godot by double clicking on the file that has just been unzipped.

LAUNCHING GODOT

- After launching Godot, a new window will be displayed as follows.

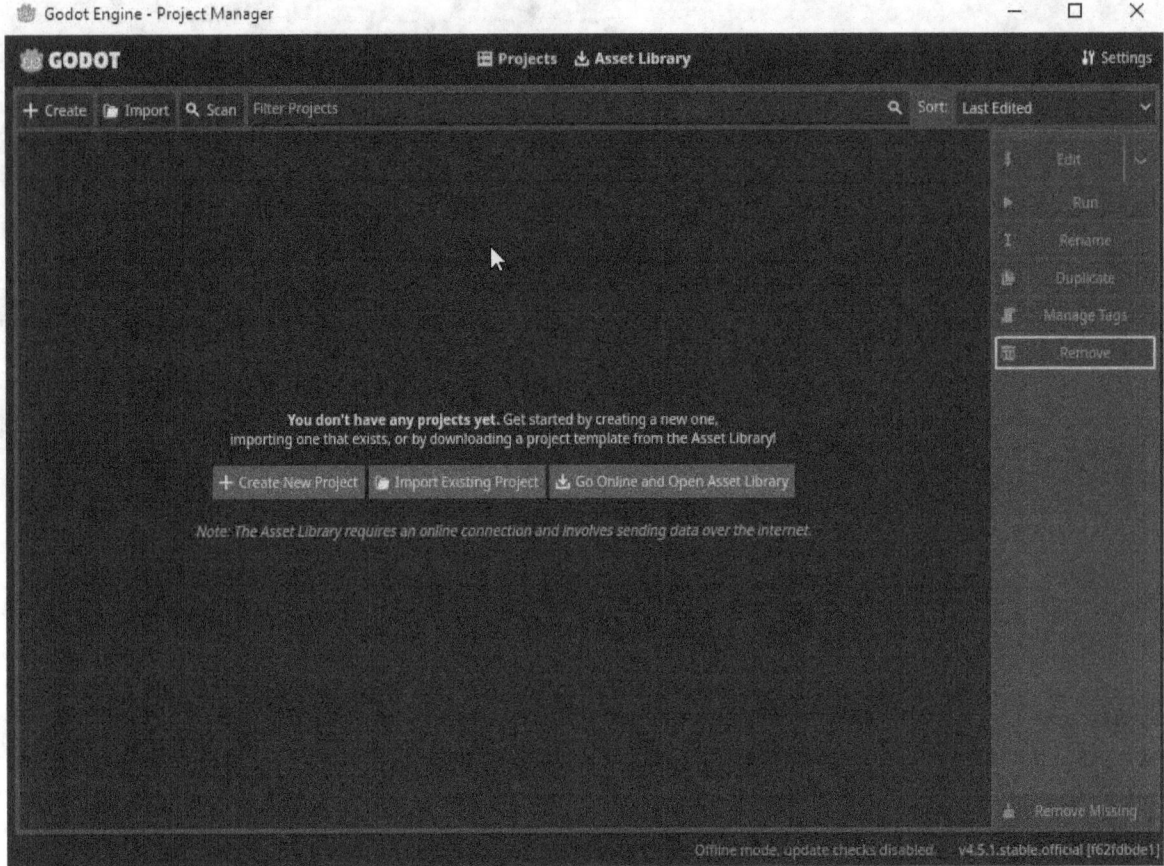

This window includes two tabs: a tab called Local **Projects** that lists all your projects and **Asset Library**.

For now, we will create a new project to become familiar with the interface.

- Click on the button labelled **Create New Project**.

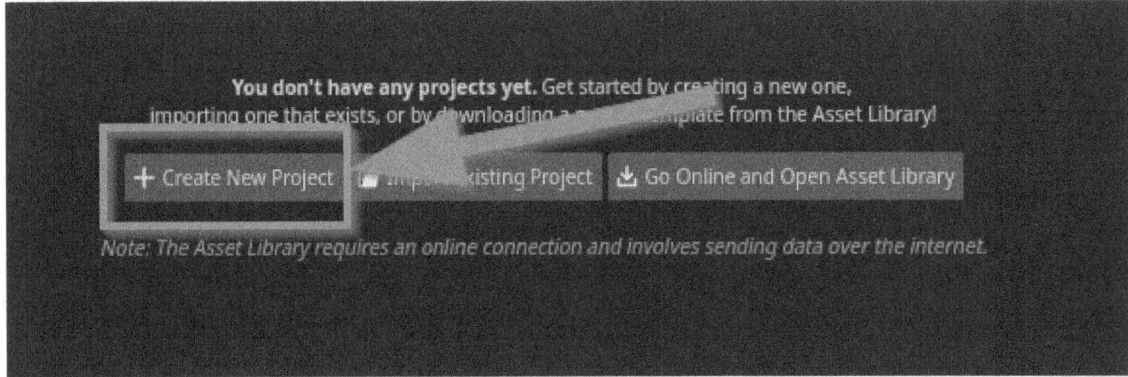

- A new window will appear as illustrated in the next figure:

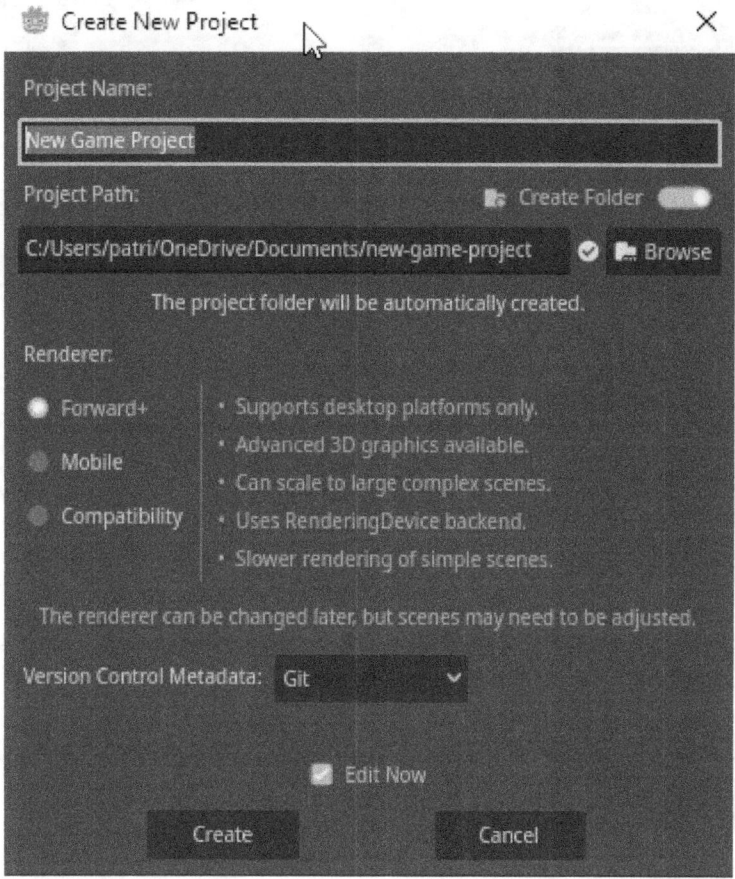

As we will see in the next steps, this window will make it possible for you to provide a name and a location for your project.

- enter a name for your project in the field labelled "**Project Name**", for example "**My First Project**".

- By default, your project will be saved in your home folder; this being said, if you prefer to save it in a different location, click on the button labelled "**Browse**" to select the location of your choice and or create a new folder.

- type the name of the new folder and click on the button labelled "**OK**".

- Once this is done, you can click on the button labelled "**Select Current Folder**" so that the folder that you have just created is used for your project.

- In the new window, you can then click on the button labelled "**Create**".

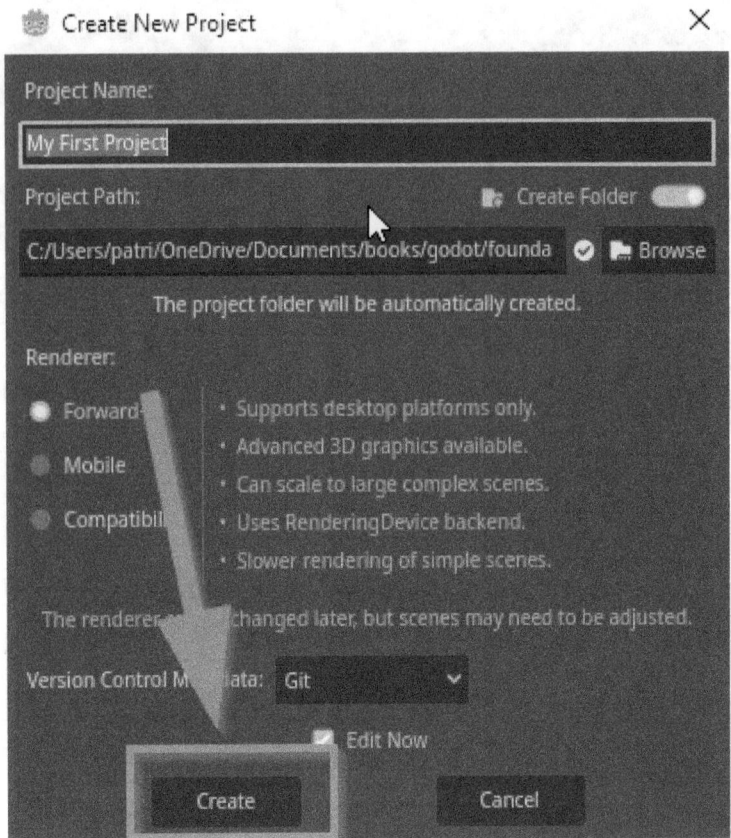

- At this stage Godot should open.

That's it, you have now installed and launched Godot. In the next section, we will start to familiarize ourselves with the different windows available in Godot.

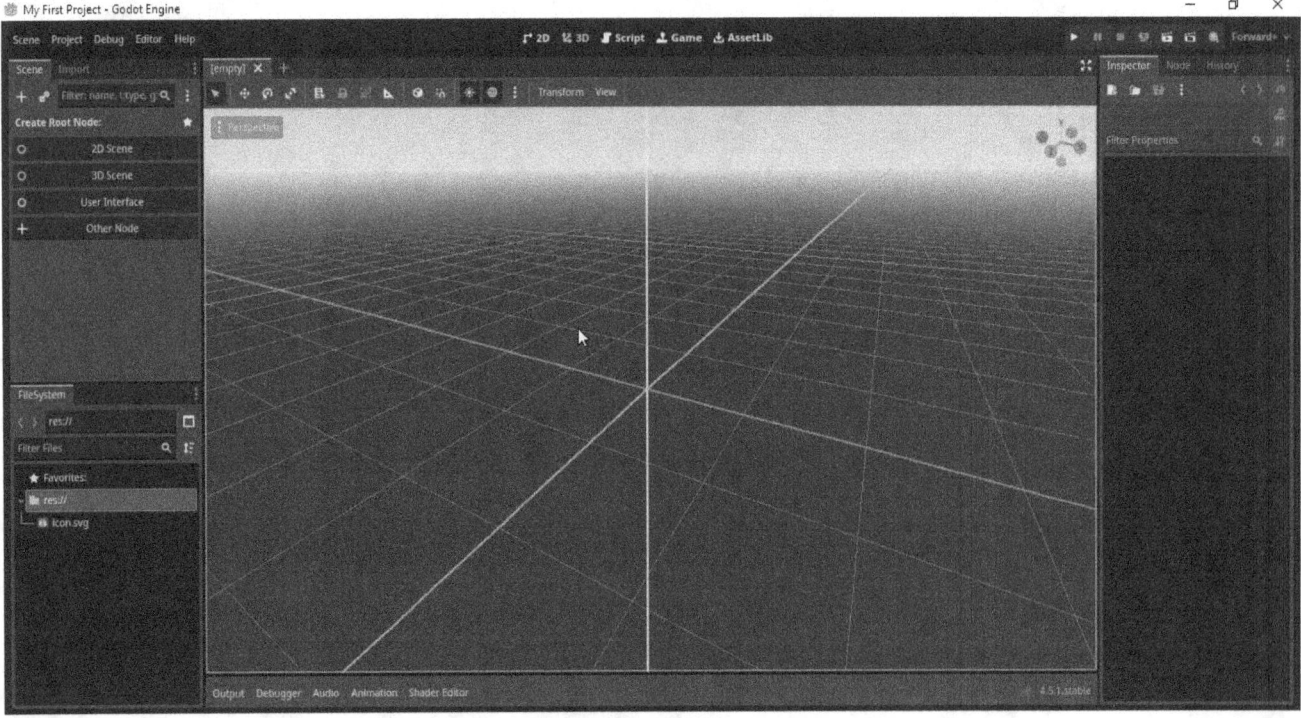

> Godot provides links to official forums and documentation from the main (i.e., top) menu: **Help | Online Documentation**

UNDERSTANDING AND BECOMING FAMILIAR WITH THE INTERFACE

After launching Godot, you will notice that it includes several windows organized in a (default) layout. Each of these windows includes a label in their top-left corner. These windows can be moved around and rearranged, if necessary, by either changing the layout (using the menu **Editor | Editor Layout | ...**) or by dragging and dropping the corresponding tab for a window to a different location. This will move the view/panel (or window) to where you would like it to appear onscreen. In the default layout, the following views appear onscreen.

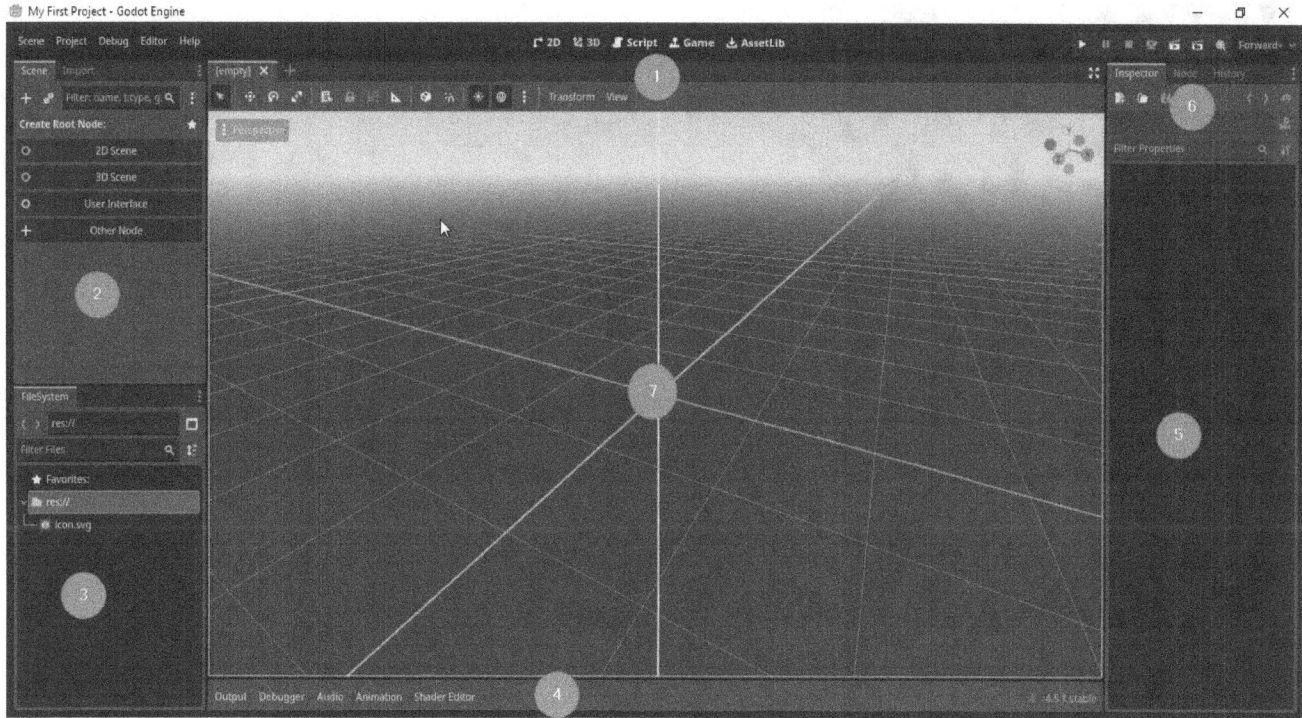

1. The top tabs: theses workspaces are used to visualize a 3D scene, or a 2D scene, the scripts included in your scene, the game as it will look when played, and the different assets that you can avail of for your project.

2. The **Scene** tab: this window or view lists all the nodes currently present in your scene. These could include, for example, basic shapes, 3D characters, or terrains. This view also makes it possible to identify a hierarchy between nodes, and to identify, for example, whether an object has children or parents (we will explore this concept later).

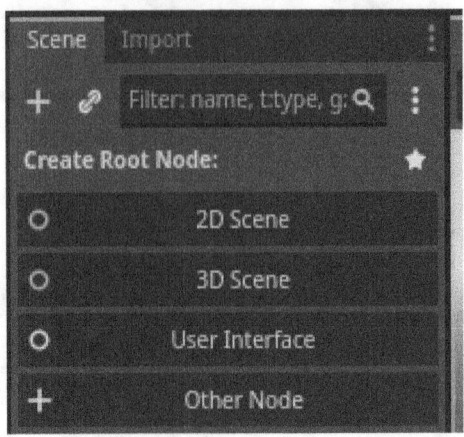

3. The **FileSystem** tab: this window includes all the assets available and used for your project, such as 3D models, sounds, or textures.

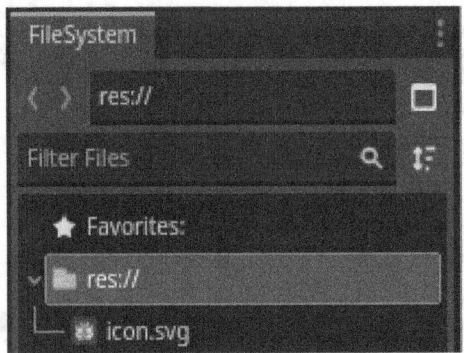

4. The bottom tabs: these tabs include information related to your actions in Godot, as well as compile errors, amongst other things. More specifically information will be related to animation, audio, compilation, messages from your code, and actions in Godot.

5. The **Inspector** tab: this tab displays information (i.e., the properties) on the object or the node that is currently selected.

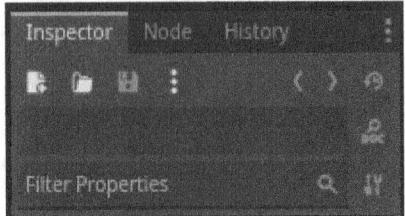

6. The Play-Test buttons (located in the top right corner): these buttons make it possible to play/pause/stop/build the current project or scene.

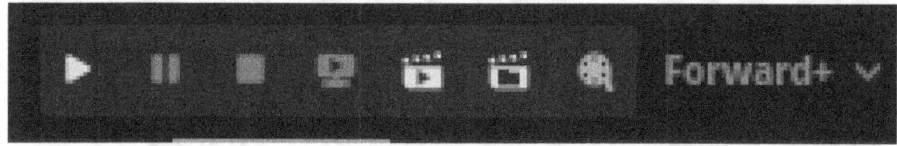

7. The **View** port: this tab located in the middle of the screen displays the content of a scene (or the item listed in the **Hierarchy** view) so that you can visualize and modify them accordingly (e.g., move, scale, etc.).

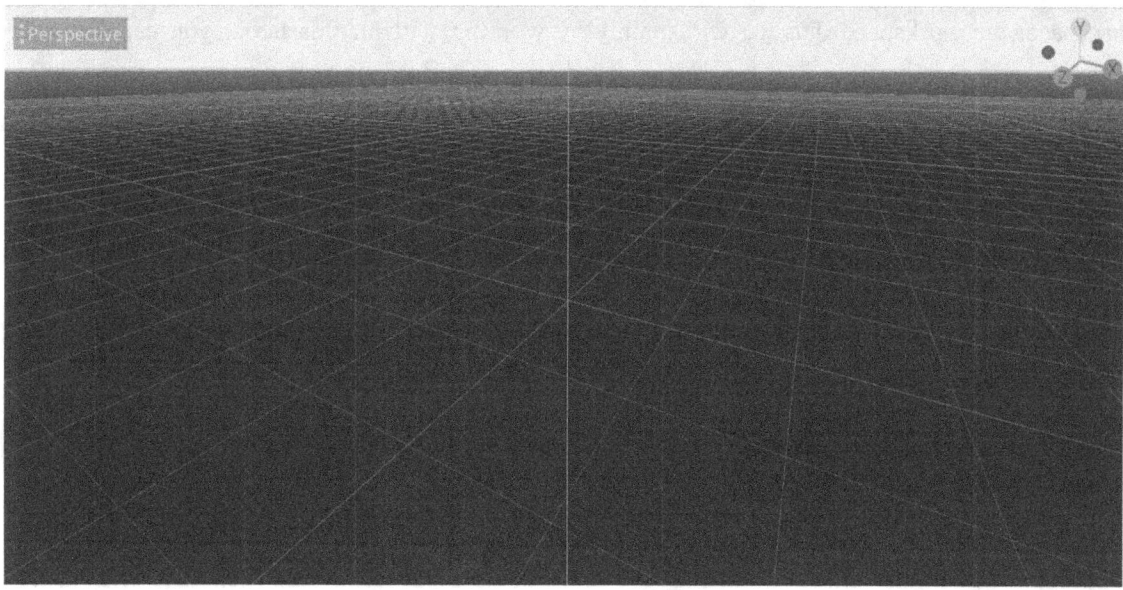

THE VIEWPORT

We will use this view to create and visualize the scene for our game. When you create a project, you can include several scenes within. A scene is comparable to a level, and scenes that are included in the same project can share similar resources, so that assets are imported once and shared across (or used in) all scenes.

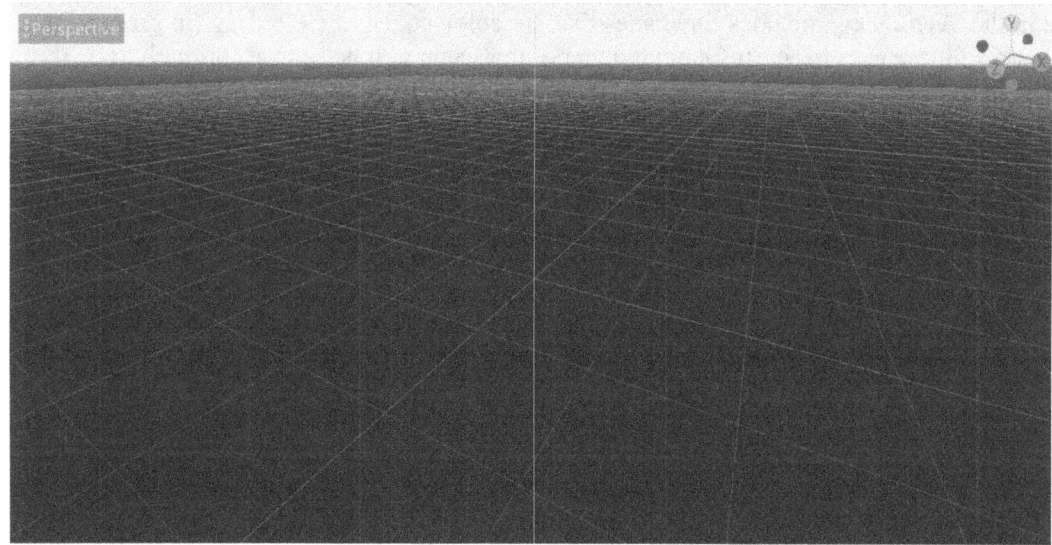

DISCOVERING AND NAVIGATING THROUGH THE SCENE

So that you can navigate easily in the current scene, several shortcuts and navigation modes are available. These make it possible to navigate through your scene just as you would in a First-Person Shooter or to literally "fly" through your scene. You can also zoom-in and zoom-out to focus on specific areas or objects, look around (i.e., using mouse look) or pan the view to focus on a specific part of the scene. The main modes of navigation are provided in the next table. However, we will look into these in more detail in the next section as we will be experimenting with them to explore (and modify) an existing scene.

In the 3D workspace, the workspace that we will mainly be working with in this book, you can navigate as follows:

- Rotate the view: Middle Mouse Button (MMB) + Drag and Drop.

- Pan the view: Middle Mouse Button (MMB) + Drag and Drop + SHIFT.

- Zoom-in and out: Mouse Wheel (MW) Forward or back.

To activate the 3D workspace, you can click on the button called 3D, at the top of the window.

As you can see, all these navigation features are very useful to navigate through your scene and to visualize all its elements. In addition, you can also choose to display the scene along a particular axis (i.e., x, y, or z) using the **gizmo** that is displayed in the top-right corner of the **Scene** view as described on the next figure.

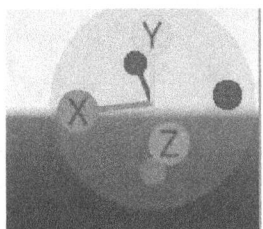

The gizmo available in the **Scene** view includes three axes that are color-coded: x (in red), y (in green) and z (in blue). By clicking on any of these axes (or corresponding letters), the scene will be seen accordingly (i.e., through the x-, y-, or z-axis).

If you are not familiar with 3D axes: **x**, and **z** usually refer to the width and depth, while **y** refers to the height. By default, in Godot, the z-axis is pointing towards you if the x-axis is pointing to the right and the y-axis is pointing upwards. This is often referred as a right-handed coordinate system.

In addition to the navigation tools, Godot also offers ways to focus on a particular node by selecting the object in the **Scene Tree**, and then pressing the key **F**.

While the shortcuts and keys described in this section should get you started with Godot and make it possible for you to navigate through your scene easily, there are, obviously, many more shortcuts that you could use, but that will not be presented in this book. Instead, you may look for and find these in the official documentation that is available both offline using the following link:

https://docs.godotengine.org/en/stable/getting_started/editor/default_key_mapping.html.

Alternatively, you can open the online help (**Help | Online Documentation**) and choose: **Manual | Editor Introduction**.

THE SCENE TREE (OR SCENE DOCK)

As indicated by its name, this dock lists and displays the name of all nodes included in the scene (in alphabetical order, by default) along with the type of relationship or hierarchy between them.

In Godot each scene is a combination of nodes organized in a tree-like structure whereby each node (except from the root node) has either a parent and/or children, and also properties that you can modify.

The **Scene Tree** offers several advantages when we need to manage all the nodes present in the scene quickly and to perform organizational changes. For example, we could use this view to find nodes based on their name, to duplicate nodes, to amend the name of nodes, to amend the properties of several nodes, or to change the hierarchy between nodes.

For example, on the following figure, we can see that:

- The scene includes seven several nested nodes: the node called **house** includes two nodes called **room1** and **room2**.

- The node called **room1** includes a node called **chair**.

- In this case the node called **house** is the parent of the nodes called **room1** and **room2**, and **room1** and **room2** are the children of their parent node called **house**.

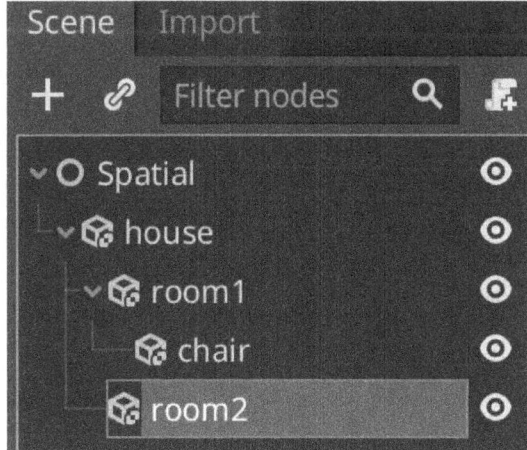

To change the hierarchy of the scene and make some nodes children of a particular node, we only need to drag these nodes atop the parent object.

THE FILESYSTEM DOCK

This dock includes and displays all the assets employed in your project (and across scenes), including audio files, textures, scripts (e.g., scripts written in C#), materials, 3D models, or scenes, or packages. All these assets, once present in the **FileSystem dock**, can be shared across scenes.

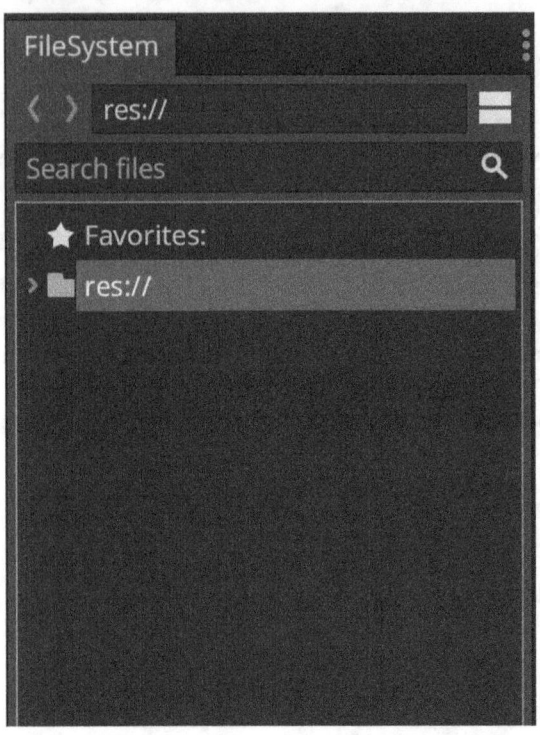

In other words, if we create a project and then a scene, and import assets for our game, these assets will be available from any other scene within the same project.

As for the **Scene Tree**, search capabilities are included to ease the management of all your assets.

By default, the **FileSystem tab** will list the files and folders included in your project along with a search field that can be used to find files and assets within your project.

THE INSPECTOR

This dock displays the properties of the node currently selected (e.g., the node selected in the **Scene Tree**) and it makes it possible to modify the attributes of a node accordingly.

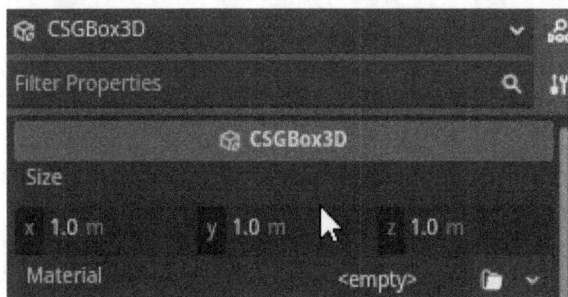

By default, all nodes present in the scene have a name; if they are Node3D nodes, they also include attributes such as **Transform** (for their position, rotation and scale attributes), a **Matrix** (another way to specify the node's location, Position and scale attributes), and **Visibility** (to specify whether they should be seen in the scene).

THE BOTTOM PANEL

The bottom panel includes tabs with information related to your actions in Godot, animation, audio, compilation, messages from your code, and actions in Godot.

- The **Output** tab will list all your actions in Godot and is comparable to a log. This tab can also be used to display messages from your code.

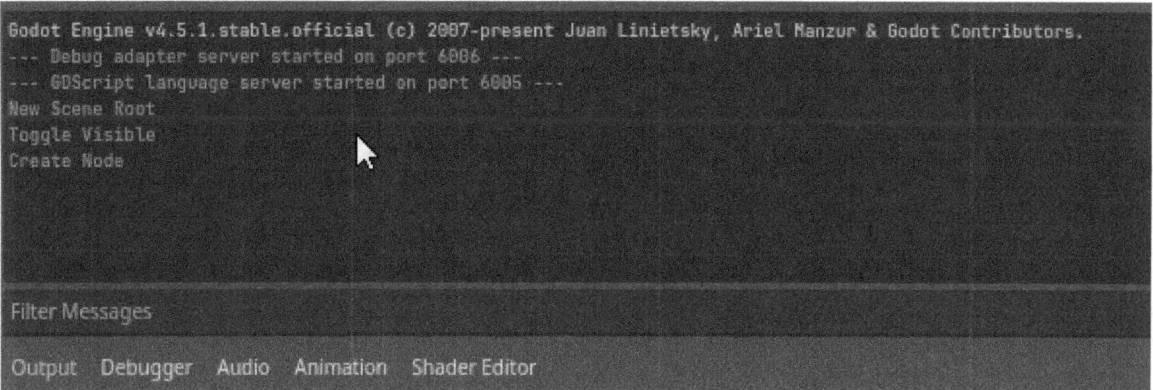

- The **Debugger** tab will be useful to see any compilation errors when you create and compile your scripts.

- The **Audio** tab will be useful to inspect and manage audio buses, levels, and effects while your game is running. It lets you see real-time audio output, adjust volumes, mute channels, and diagnose audio issues. This is especially helpful when balancing sound effects, music, and UI feedback.

- The **Animation** tab will be useful to create, edit, and preview animations for your characters, UI, or objects. It gives you a timeline where you can keyframe properties such as position, rotation, scale, and sprite frames. This is essential when building smooth motion and interactions in your game.

- The **Shader Editor** tab will be useful to write, edit, and debug custom shaders directly inside Godot. It provides a text editor with syntax highlighting and real-time preview of the shader's effect. This is perfect for creating visual effects like glowing objects, water, fire, and custom materials

THE ASSET LIBRARY

This window, which is not displayed by default when you open Godot, connects you to the **Asset Library**, an online repository where you can search for and find assets for your game. All these assets are free of charge which makes it like a software repository.

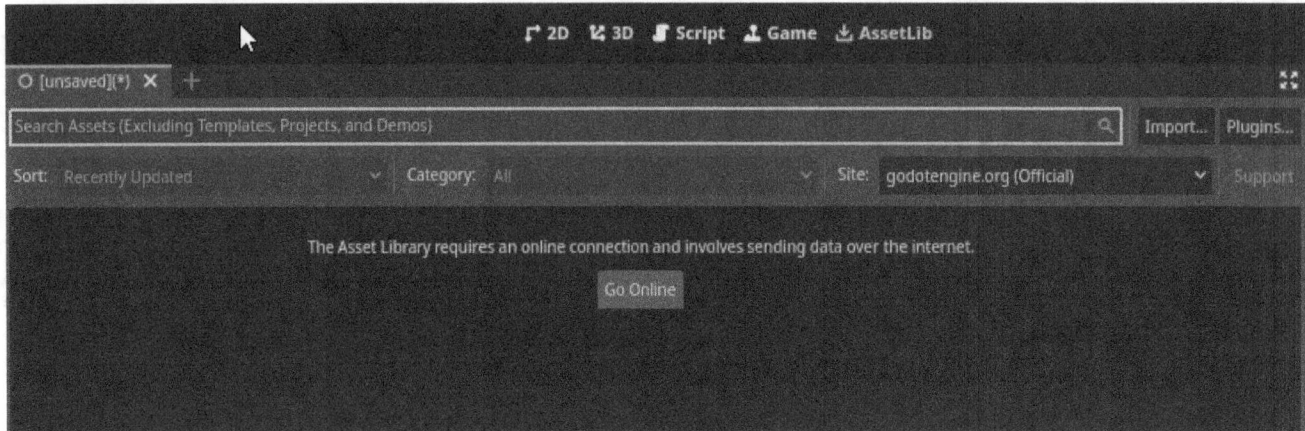

- After clicking on the button labelled "Go Online" the screen will display the assets available online:

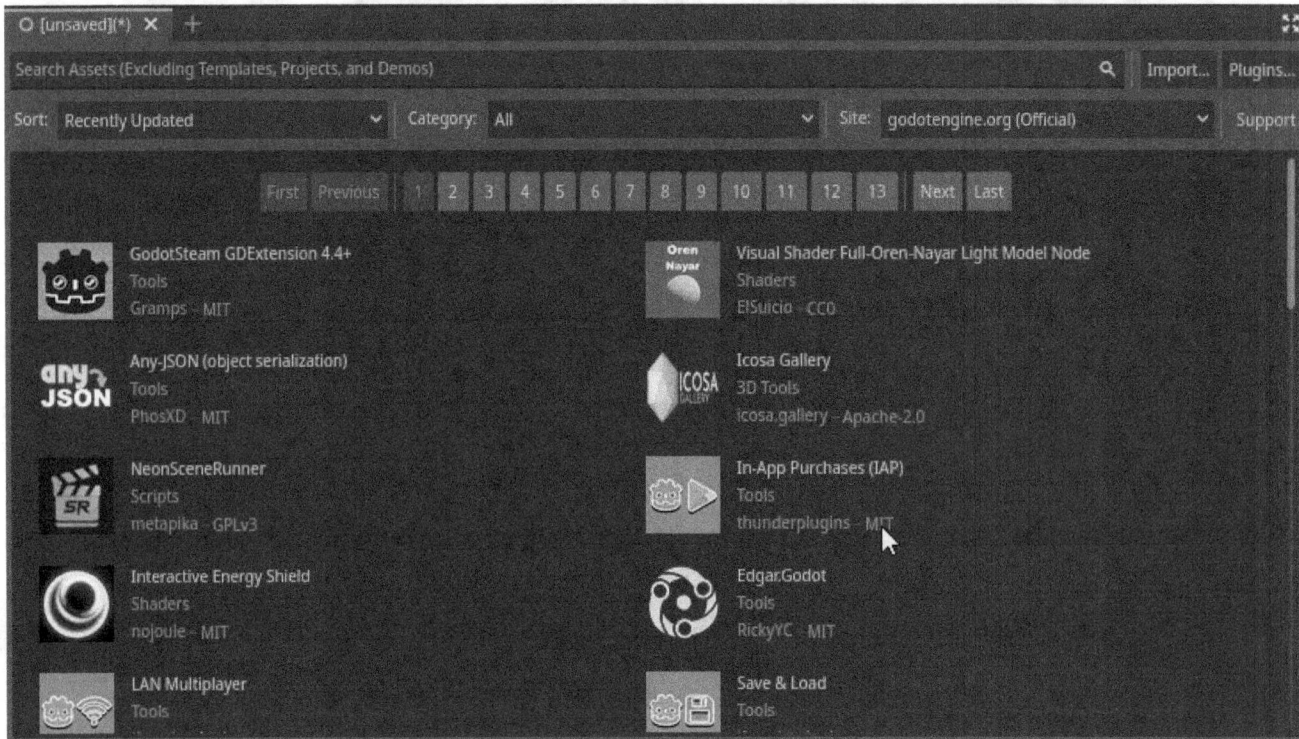

LEVEL ROUNDUP

Summary

In this chapter, we have become familiar with the different views and windows available in Godot. We also looked at how to navigate through scenes and how to change the layout of our working environment. In the next chapter, we will harness these skills to be able to create and navigate through our own 3D environment.

Quiz

It is now time to test your knowledge. specify whether the following statements are TRUE or FALSE. The answers are available on the next page.

1. To install Godot, you need to launch an installer.

2. Godot is premium software.

3. With Godot you can create both 2D and 3D games.

4. In Godot, you can specify where your project will be saved.

5. Once an asset has been downloaded in the scene, it is not available in other scenes within the same project.

6. It is possible to make some nodes invisible in Godot.

7. To make some nodes children of other nodes, you can select a node and drag and drop it atop its parent.

8. Godot is using a right-hand coordinate system.

9. Help on Godot is available online.

10. To rotate the current view in the 3D mode you can use the Middle Mouse Button and drag and drop your mouse.

Solutions to the Quiz

1. FALSE.

2. FALSE.

3. TRUE.

4. TRUE.

5. FALSE.

6. TRUE.

7. TRUE.

8. TRUE.

9. TRUE.

10. TRUE.

Checklist

If you can do the following, then you are ready to go to the next chapter:

- Install Godot.

- Navigate through a scene easily.

- Pan or rotate the view in a 3D mode.

- Answer at least 7 out of 10 of the questions correctly in the quiz.

CHAPTER 3: CREATING AND EXPORTING YOUR FIRST SCENE

In this chapter, we will create our first scene and start to include, combine, and apply textures to basic shapes such as boxes. This chapter explains how to use basic transformations and how to apply them to objects. It will also explain how to manage and group objects.

After completing this section, you should be able to:

- Create a scene.

- Add basic objects.

- Create and apply colors and textures to objects.

- Group shapes.

- Search for particular objects or assets using shortcuts.

- Export your first scene.

CREATING A NEW PROJECT AND A NEW SCENE

Now that we have covered the main features for the interface, we will create a simple scene that you can navigate through and that includes textures and colors for some of these objects.

After completing this section, you will be able to:

- Add basic objects to your scene.

- Apply basic texturing and coloring to objects.

- Transform objects (i.e., move, scale, and rotate objects).

- Add a character controller to the scene to be able to walk around the level.

- Add and configure lights.

- Group objects and apply attributes to several objects at a time.

ADDING AND COMBINING SIMPLE BUILT-IN OBJECTS TO YOUR SCENE

As we will see later, we can create our game environment using a wide range of primitive shapes (e.g., cylinders, spheres, boxes, etc.), lights (e.g., directional lights or point lights), cameras, and other built-in assets (e.g., character controllers). Once these objects have been added to the current scene, Godot makes it possible to modify their attributes.

First let's configure our scene so that we can create 3D content.

- In the **Scene Tree** tab, you should see a message asking you to create a **Root Node**.

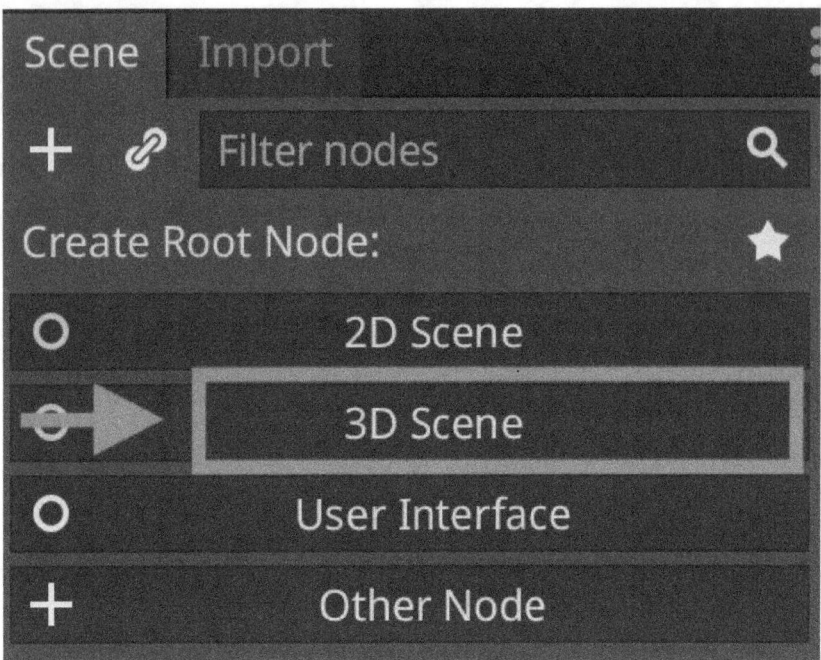

- Click on the option "**3D Scene**" as we will be creating a 3D scene for now.

After selecting this option, the **Scene Tree** should display a node called **Node3D**. This node will be the basis for the rest of our scene.

Next, let's create a cube that will be used for the ground:

- right-click on the node called **Node3D**.

- From the contextual menu, select the option **Add Child Node**.

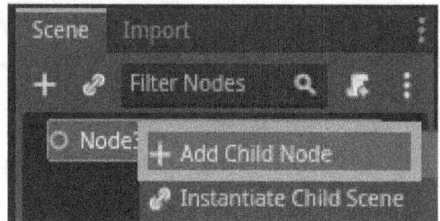

- In the new window, type the word **box** in the search field.

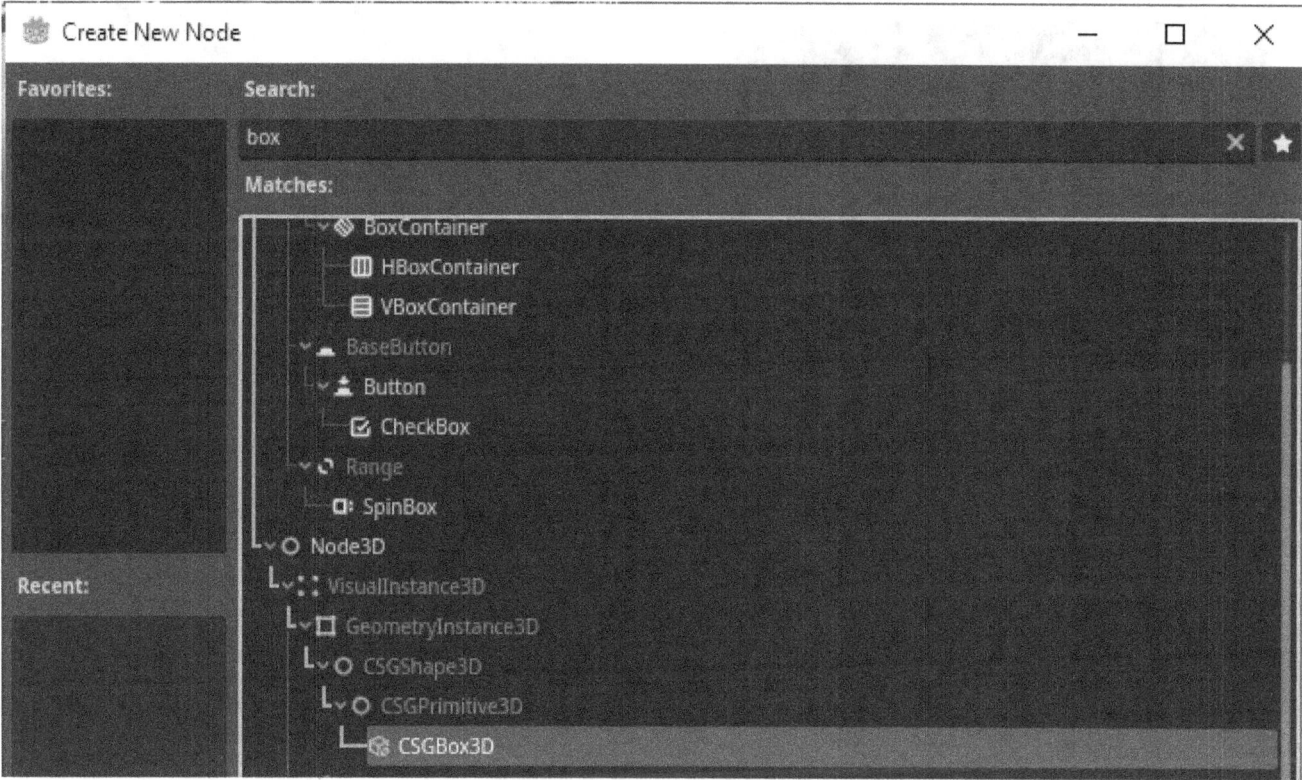

- You can then select (double click) on the node type called **CSGBox3D**.

- This will create a box that will be, by default, located at the position **(0, 0, 0)** with a size of **1**. This means that the height, depth, and width of this object are equal to 1.

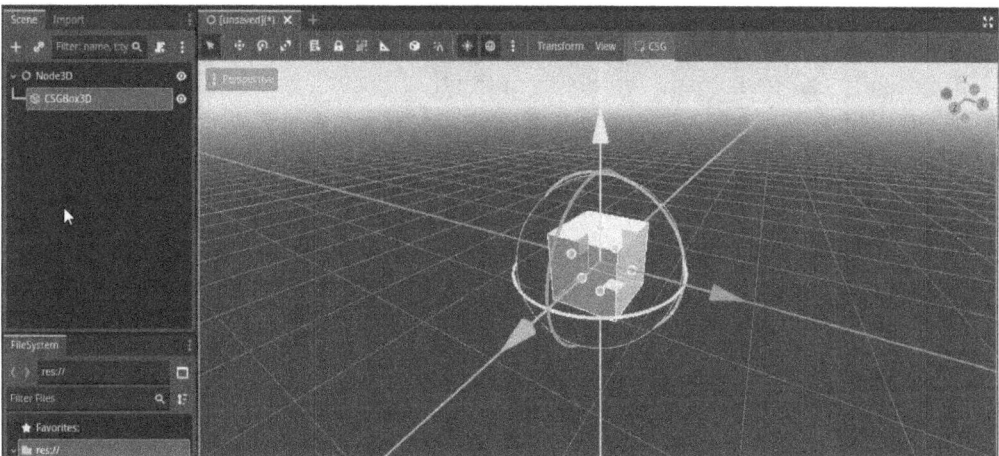

- rename the cube **myCube**: to rename the cube, we can (1) select it in the **Scene Tree** and then press **CTRL + ENTER** simultaneously, or (2) select it in the **Scene Tree** and double click on it, or (3) right-click on the object in the **Scene Tree** window and select the option **Rename** from the contextual menu.

Once you have renamed the cube, we can change some of its properties and see how this affects its appearance. For example:

- In the **Inspector** window, locate the attribute called **Transform**, and change the **x**, **y**, and **z scale** properties to **2** and see how it affects the size of the cube.

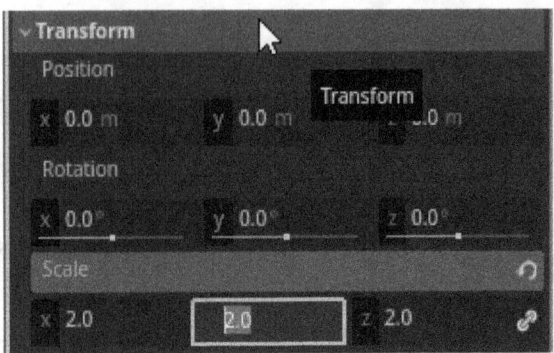

Note that you can use the search box located at the top of the **Inspector** window to look for a specific attribute.

- Change its **y** rotation attributes to **45** (i.e., a rotation around the y-axis expressed in degrees), and see how its orientation has changed. Note that for any of these parameters, you can use the **Inspector** window to either change a value in the corresponding text fields or click on one of the parameters and drag and drop the mouse: this will either increase or decrease the value in the corresponding field. It is usually an easier way to amend the attributes of an object.

Once you are comfortable with modifying the **transform** properties of the cube using the **Inspector**, let's look at other interesting ways to observe the objects and the scene to modify their attributes.

You will notice a toolbar located in the top-left corner of the viewport, as illustrated in the next figure.

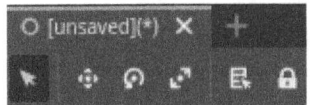

This toolbar includes, amongst other things, three distinct buttons that are shortcuts to (from left to right) select the object, move the object currently selected, rotate the object currently selected, or scale the object currently selected. These three buttons can also be accessed using the key shortcuts Q, *W, E,* and *R*.

Before we transform this object, let's experiment with the **Panning** and rotating the view:

- Rotating around the object: press the **Middle Mouse Button** and **drag and drop** the mouse; you should see that you are effectively rotating the view around the selected object.

- Panning the view: press the **Middle Mouse Button** and the **SHIFT** key and drag and drop the mouse; you should see that you are effectively panning the view.

- Focusing the view on the object currently selected: press the **key F** and you should see that the view is now re-focused on the current object selected.

- Zooming: move the mouse wheel and check that you can zoom in and out

Before we look at how to transform our cube, let's look at a useful widget called a **gizmo**. This widget, illustrated on the next figure, is located in the top-right corner of the **Scene** view and makes it possible to view the scene from several axes and perspectives.

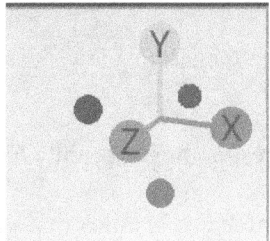

Using the gizmo

Using this gizmo, and by clicking on its **x**, **y**, or **z** arms, we can see the scene from the corresponding axis. Let's experiment with it:

- We can successively click on the **x**, **y**, and **z** arms of the gizmo, and see how the view changes.

- Note that by clicking on the button labelled **Perspective** (top-left corner), you can switch between the perspective and orthographic (or isometric) views.

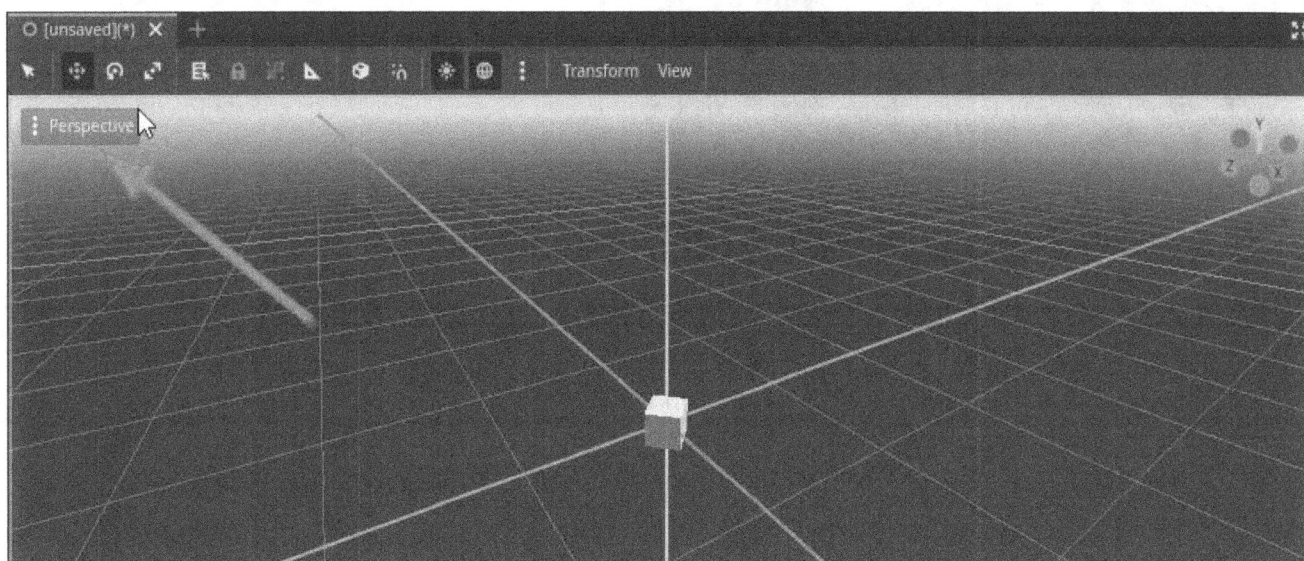

- To readjust the view, we can press the **Middle Mouse Button** and **drag and drop** the mouse, so that we can rotate around the object accordingly.

After this short distraction, let's come back to our top-left toolbar and experiment with the three buttons dedicated to transform nodes.

First, let's experiment with the **Move** tool:

- Select the **Move** tool from the toolbar or use the corresponding shortcut (**W**).

- You should now see three arrows from the cube. These arrows are handles that you can drag and drop to move the selected object in a particular direction (e.g., along the x-, y- or z-axis).

As you successively drag the blue, red, and green handles, observe how you can move your object along the corresponding axes.

Now, let's experiment with the **Rotation** tool:

- Select the object called "**myCube**" in the **Scene Tree**, and press the key **F** to focus the view on this object.

- Select the **Rotation** tool from the toolbar (third icon from the left) or use the corresponding shortcut (**E**).

You should now see a combination of green, red, and blue circles around the object. These are handles that you can drag and drop to rotate the object currently selected around a particular axis (e.g., around the x-, y- and z-axis).

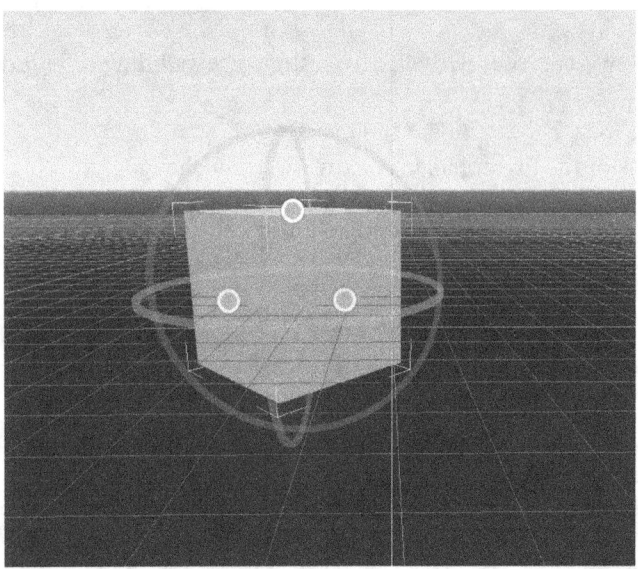

The color of the handle indicates the axis around which the object will be rotated. For example, by dragging and dropping the green handle, we can rotate the object around the y-axis. The same applies to the blue and red handles for a rotation around the z-axis or x-axis, respectively.

As we drag these handles, we can see that the values for the corresponding **Rotation** attributes in the **Inspector** also change.

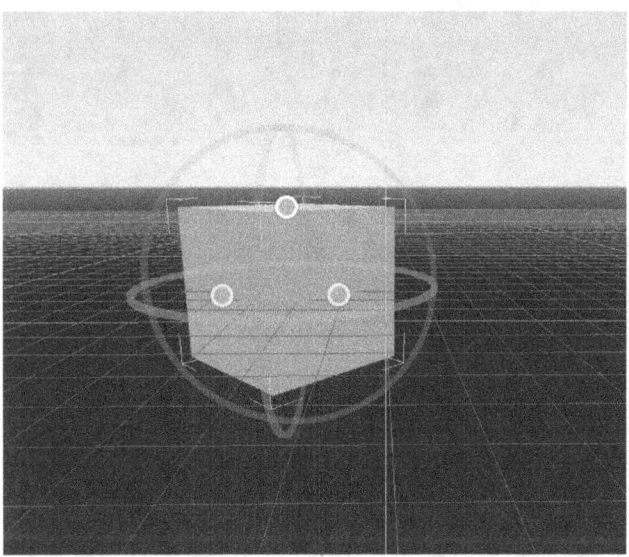

Now, let's experiment with the **Scale** tool:

- Select the **Scale** tool from the toolbar (fourth icon from the left) or use the corresponding shortcut (**R**).

- You should now see a combination of green, red, and blue lines and handles around the object. These are handles that you can drag and drop to scale the selected object along a particular axis (e.g., along the x-, y-, and z-axis).

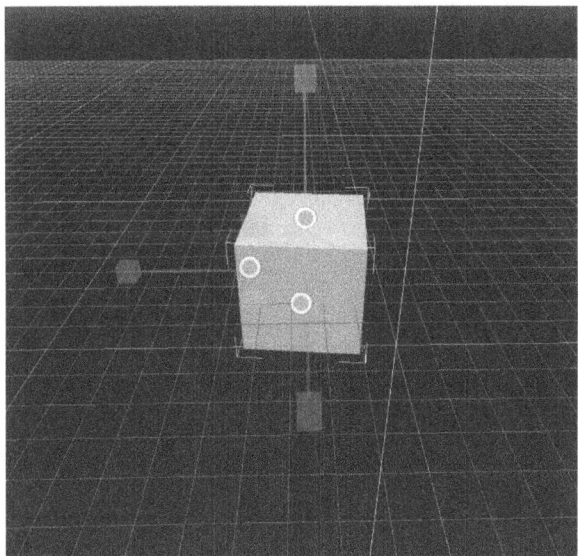

The color of the handle indicates the axis along which the object will be scaled. For example, by dragging and dropping the green handle, we can scale the object along the y-axis. The same applies to the blue (z-axis) and red (x-axis) handles. Also note that by dragging the middle white square, the transformation will be uniform. In other words, the amount of scaling will be the same on all three axes (x-, y-, and z-axis).

At this stage, we have performed several transformations on the new cube, and we may want to reset its attributes so that it is the same as when it was initially created. We can do so by using the round arrow located to the right of the attributes **Position**, **Rotation** and **Scale**, as described on the next figure.

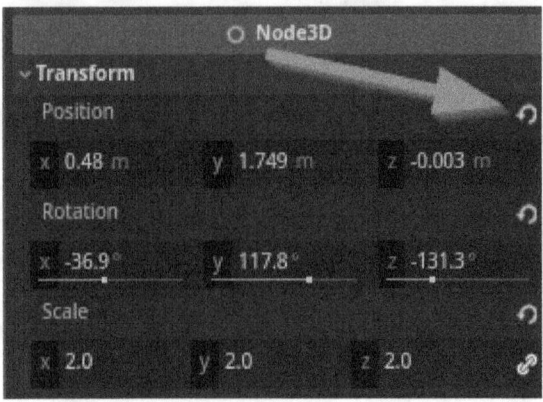

For more information and tips on how to use Godot's interface, you can check Godot's official documentation.

ADDING COLORS AND TEXTURES

At this stage we have a box in our scene that we can see through the viewport; this being said, it would be great to add two other objects to our scene: a camera so that we can preview our scene, and also lights.

Before we start adding colors and texture, let's reset the box to its original size and set its scale attribute to **(1, 1, 1)**:

- Select the box in the **Scene Tree**.

- Using the **Inspector**, locate the attribute called **Transform**.

- Set the **Position** attribute to **(0, 0, 0)** and the **Scale** attribute to **(1, 1, 1)**.

- Note that to reset one of these attributes, you can also click on the revolving arrow to the right of each attribute, as illustrated in the next figure.

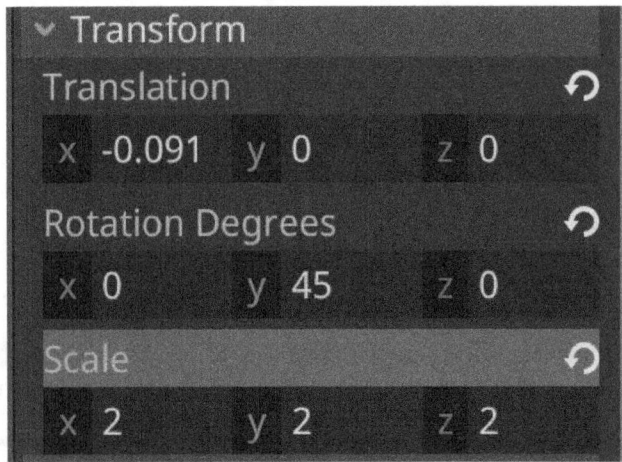

Now that we have reset the transform attributes of the box, let's add a camera:

- Select the node called **Node3D** in the **Scene Tree**.

- Right-click on it and select **Add Child Node** from the contextual menu. This means that the new camera that we have created will be a child of the root node called **Node3D**.

- In the new window, type the word **camera** in the search field, and then select (i.e., double click on) the node type **Camera3D** from the list.

- This will create a new node called **Camera3D** in the **Scene Tree**.

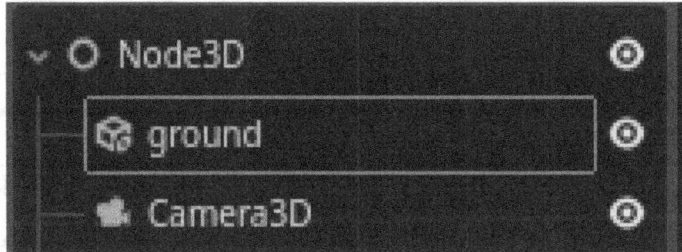

- Now that this camera has been added, you should see an option called **Preview** in the view port, as illustrated in the next figure.

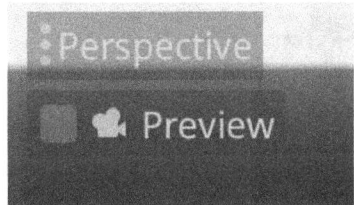

- This option makes it possible to see the scene through the lenses of the camera as a preview.

- Click on the tick box to the right of the **Preview** icon, this should display the preview as illustrated in the next figure.

This is how your game will look like. At the moment, we can only see a blue sky within the preview window, as the camera is not pointing at the box that we have created earlier. We can also see that the **Inspector** window, which is located to the right of the screen, displays the attributes of this camera.

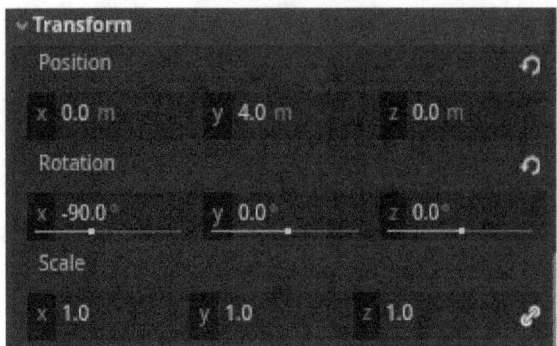

Amongst other things, we see that the camera is located at the position (**x=0, y=0, z=0**) and that it has not been rotated yet.

note that it is possible to simultaneously display the viewport and the view from one camera present in the scene by either selecting **View | 2 ViewPorts** or by pressing **CMD/CTRL + 2**, as illustrated in the next figure.

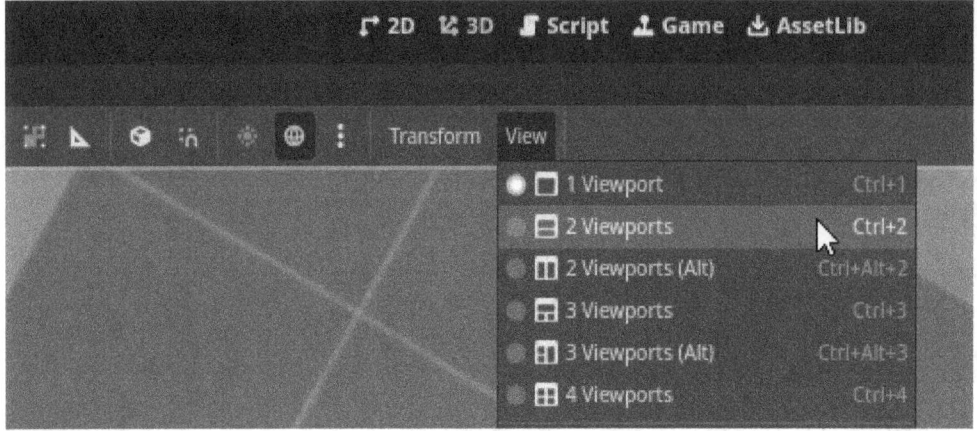

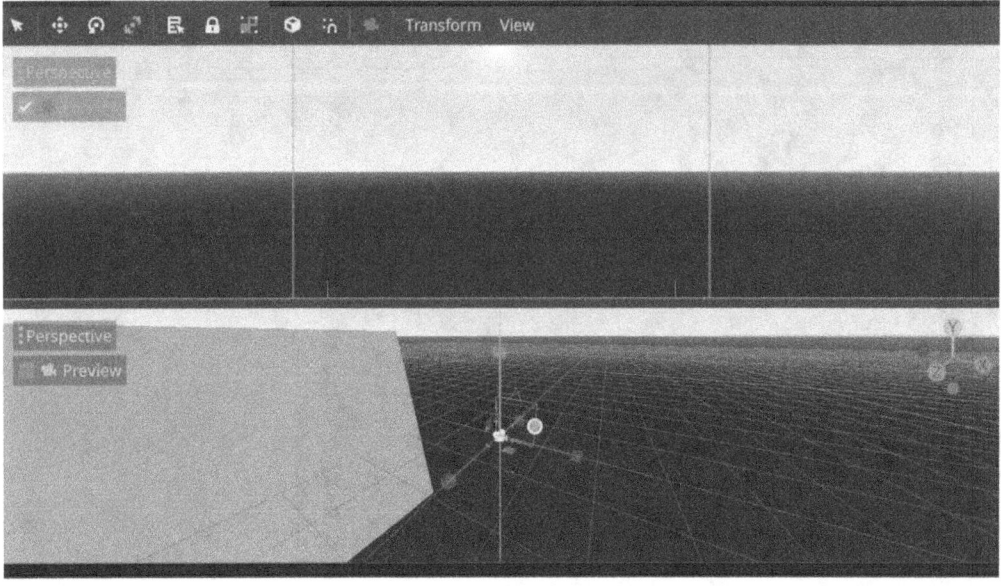

Next, we can add a light to our scene:

- Deactivate the **Preview** mode by unticking the box to the left of the **Preview** icon.

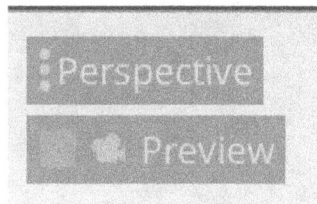

- Create a new node of type **DirectionalLight3D** that is a child of the node called **Node3D**: right-click on the node **Node3D**, select **Add Child Node** from the contextual menu, type **directionallight** in the search field, and select the type **DirectionalLight3D** from the contextual menu.

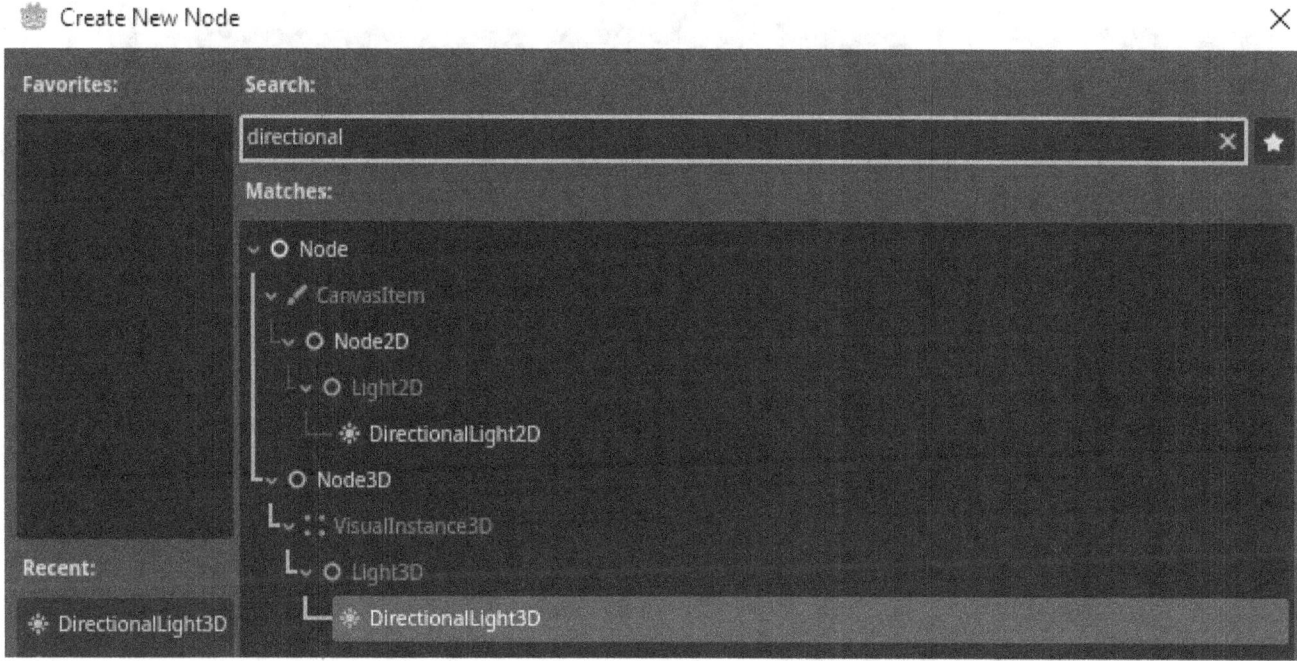

- Rename this light **myLight.**

Once this is done, we will change the orientation and position of the light so that it is above the cube and pointing downwards.

- check that its **Position** and **Rotation** parameters are set to (**0, 0, 0**).

- We can now move the light along the **y-axis** so that it is above the cube (e.g., by using the **Move** tool), for example, at the position (**0, 3, 0**).

- We can also rotate the light **-90** degrees around the **x-axis** using the **Inspector**: set the **Rotation** attribute to (**-90, 0, 0**).

- If we use the **gizmo** to see the scene along the **x-axis**, we can clearly see that the light is effectively pointing downwards, as illustrated in the next figure.

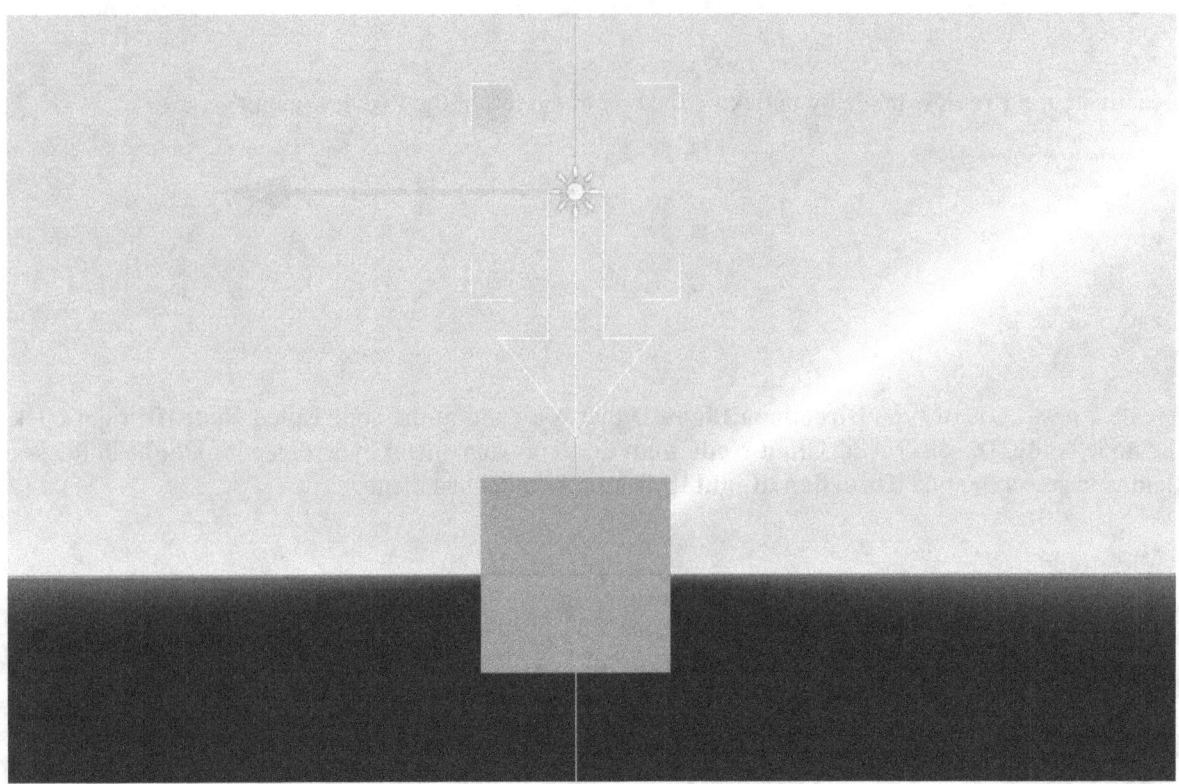

Once you are happy with the position of the light, you can rotate the view to see this object from different angles, and also look at the scene from the preview.

At this stage, our light is set-up as well as the cube. However, we would like the camera present in our scene to look at the cube from above. We will, accordingly, change the attributes of the camera to implement this feature using the **Inspector**. Note that we could also add multiple cameras to the scene, and display the image captured by these in different areas of the screen, and we will see this feature later in this book.

- select the **Camera** in the **Scene Tree** dock, as described on the next figure.

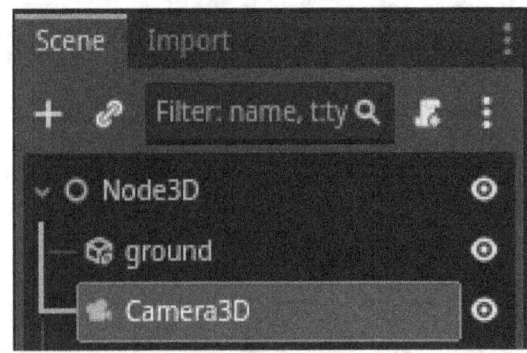

Selecting the default camera

So that it is above the cube and pointing downwards, let's change its transform settings as follows:

- **Position: (0, 4, 0)**: we raise the camera four meters above the ground.

- **Rotation: (-90, 0, 0)**: we rotate the camera -90 degrees around the x-axis.

Once these changes have been made, the scene should look as illustrated on the next figure. You may notice that, in the main viewport, the camera object is symbolized by a camera, and that its field of view is symbolized by what looks like a pyramid, which encompasses the cube in our scene. This means that the cube is in the field of view of the camera. We can check this in the camera preview window located in the bottom-right corner of the **ViewPort**.

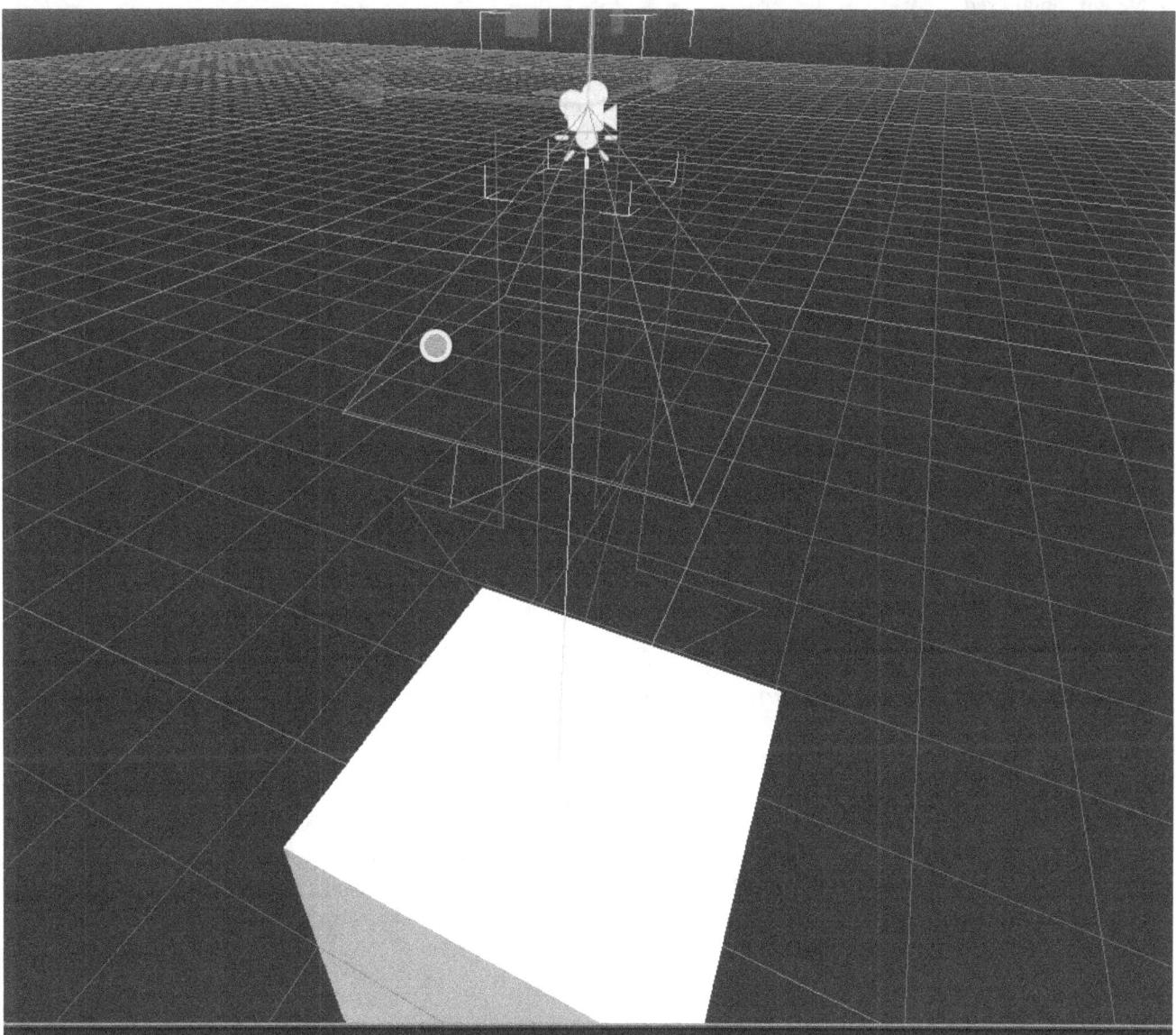

Once the camera has been configured, let's modify the attributes of the light. We will essentially change its color as well as its intensity, so that you can see how these can be amended:

- select the light called **myLight** in the **Scene Tree**.

- In the **Inspector**, you may notice an attribute called **Light**, which includes all the attributes (except for the **Transform** attributes) of the light. Click on the rectangle to the right of the label **Color**. This will make it possible to modify the color of the light. This may be useful when you need to set the atmosphere in your game and add lights of different colors.

- Once you have clicked on this rectangle, a window labeled **Color** appears. This window is similar to the one used in image manipulation software, such as Gimp or Photoshop, whereby you can pick or define a color based on its RGB code.

For those not familiar with the RGB code, its stands for Red, Green, and Blue and it can be perceived as a palette where we specify the amount of red, green, and blue that will be used to create a new color. In this window, the amount of each color is a number that ranges between 0 and 255. Which means that if we use (R=255, G=0, B=0) we will obtain red.

- If we click inside the color window, and choose a color, we can see how the RGB components change accordingly. You can choose a color of your choice, for example a light blue.

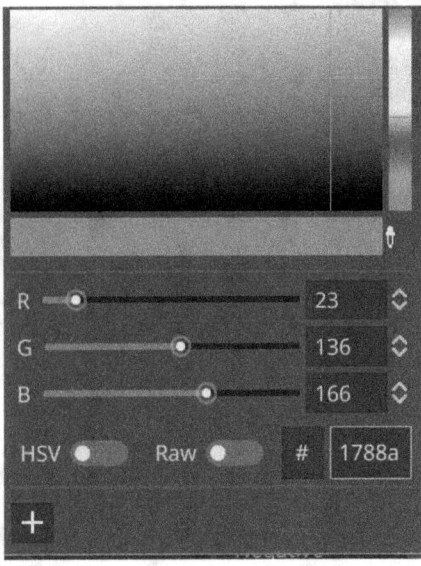

Once you have changed the color of the light, you should see that the box will turn to blue. The same will apply if we switch to the **Preview** window.

Creating the ground from a box

So far, we have a cube, a camera, and a (slightly blue) light in our scene. However, we would like to build a scene where a character walks on the ground and possibly jumps on boxes or walks up the stairs. The first step in creating this environment will be to create the ground. To do so, we can recycle the box that we have already created by modifying both its size and its appearance as follows:

- Select the box labeled **myCube.**

- Change its **scale** properties to **(40, 1, 40)**. This means that we scale it up along the x- and z-axes by **40**.

- Rename this box **ground** using the **Scene Tree**.

Now that we have resized the ground, it would be great to texture it for more realism. For this, we will set a new material for this box based on a texture that is included in your resource pack.

- Select the object called **ground**.

- Using the **Inspector**, locate the section called **CSGBox3D**, and click on the downward arrow to the right of the attribute called **Material**.

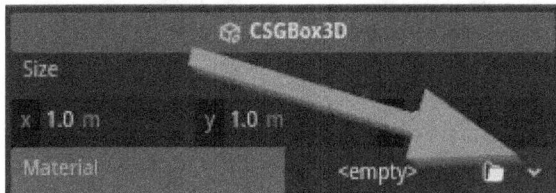

- From the contextual menu, select **StandardMaterial3D**; this means that we will create a new material that will be applied to a 3D object.

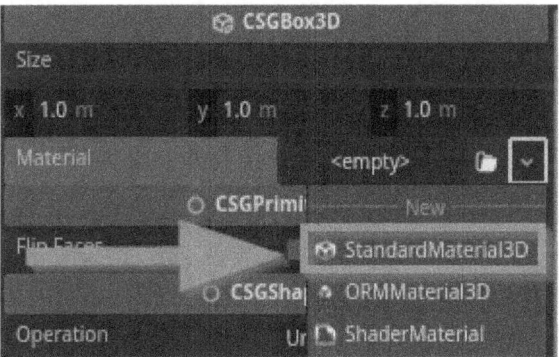

- You should now see a sphere, displayed in that section, as illustrated on the next figure.

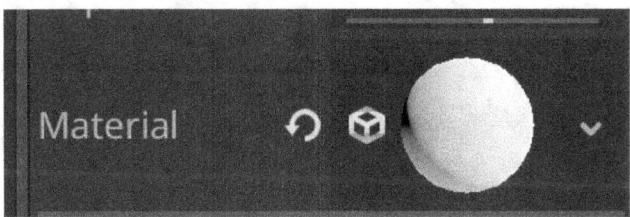

- Once you see this sphere, click on it, this should display a list of the properties for the material that you have created.

- Scroll down, and click on the parameter called **Albedo**, this will display a white rectangle to the right of the parameter along with an option to add a texture. This gives you the choice to select a new color or a texture for the ground.

- For now, we will specify a texture for the ground, so drag and drop the texture called **tile** from the resource pack to the **FileSystem** dock.

- Once the texture called **tile.jpg** appears in the **FileSystem** dock, it means that it has been imported in your project.

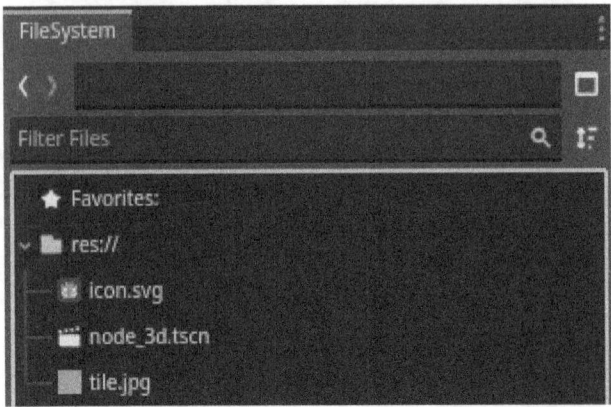

- Drag and drop this texture from the **FileSystem** dock to the attribute called texture for the box, as illustrated in the next figure.

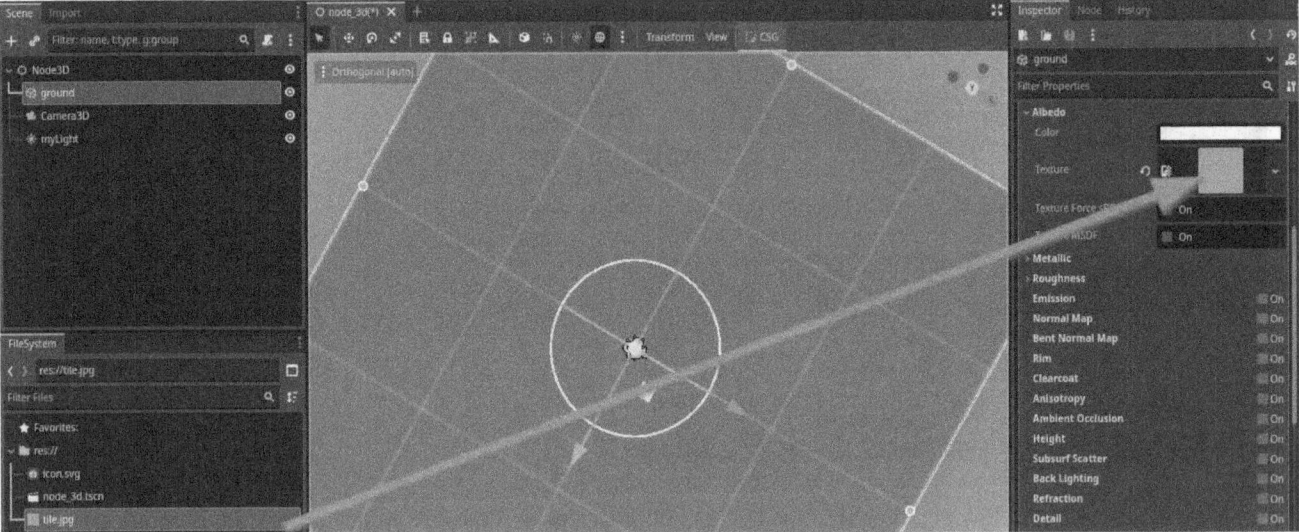

- Looking at the viewport, you should now see that the texture has been applied to the **ground** object.

- If you look closely, you will see that this texture is repeated only once on the surface of the ground.

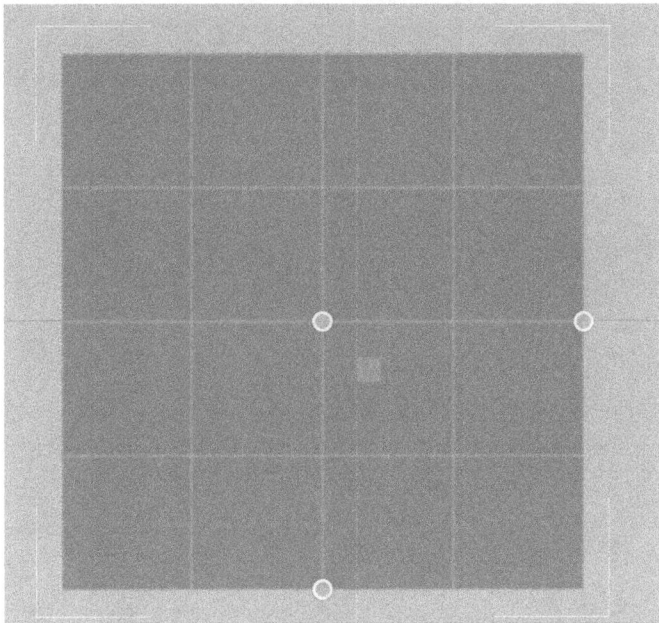

To change this and so that the pattern is repeated (or tiled) more often, we can do the following:

- Select the object called **ground** in the **Scene Tree**.

- In the **Inspector**, locate the section called **CSGBox3D**

- Click on the sphere to the right of the label **Material**.

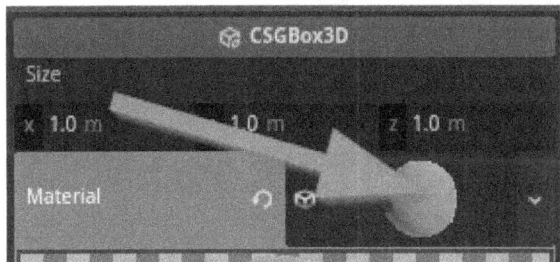

- Locate the section called **UV1** and change the **Scale** property to **(5, 5, 5)**.

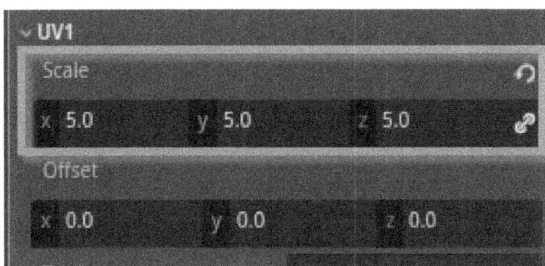

- After making these modifications, we can zoom-in to look closer at the ground.

- You should now see, in the **ViewPort**, that the pattern is tiled more often.

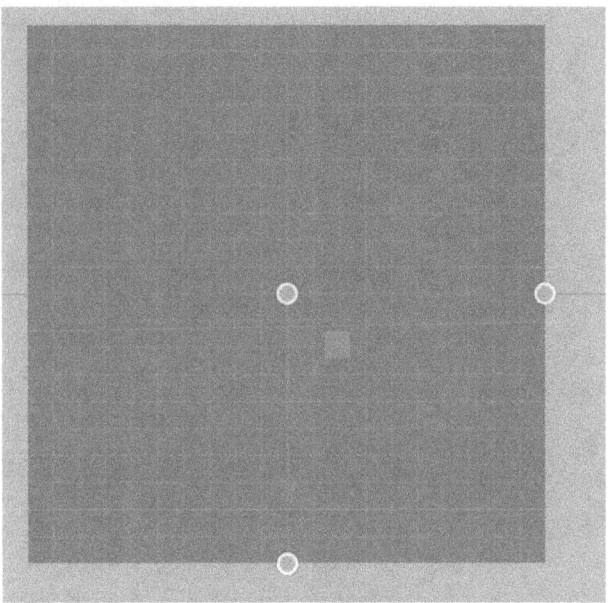

Adding multicolour boxes and stairs

Before we add new objects to the scene, let's modify the attributes of the light, so that it illuminates the scene:

- Select the light labeled **myLight.**
- Change its energy attribute (within the **Light** section) to **6** using the **Inspector** window.
- Change its **y** coordinate to **10.**

Once this is done, we will add a succession of boxes using essentially duplications to speed up the process:

- Create a new cube: right-click on the node called **Node3D**, then select **Add Child Node**, type the word **box** in the search field and select the node type **CSGBox3D**.

- Rename this cube **redBox** (e.g., in the **Scene Tree** window or in the **Inspector**).

- Change the **y** coordinate (position) of this cube so that it is above the ground; for example, you can use the position **(0, 1, 0)**.

We will now add a color to this cube, using a similar process as for the ground texture:

- Using the **Inspector**, locate the section called **CSGBox3D**, and click on the downward arrow to the right of the attribute called **Material**.

- From the contextual menu, select **StandardMaterial3D**; this means that we will create a new material that will be applied to a 3D object.

- You should now see a sphere, displayed in that section, as illustrated on the next figure.

- Once you see this sphere, click on it, this should display a list of the properties for the material that you have created.

- click on the parameter called **Albedo**, this will display a white rectangle to the right of the parameter along with an option to add a texture. This gives you the choice to select either a new color or a texture for the ground;

- Click on the white rectangle to the right of the label called **Color**.

- As the color window appears, select a red color and close the **Color** window.

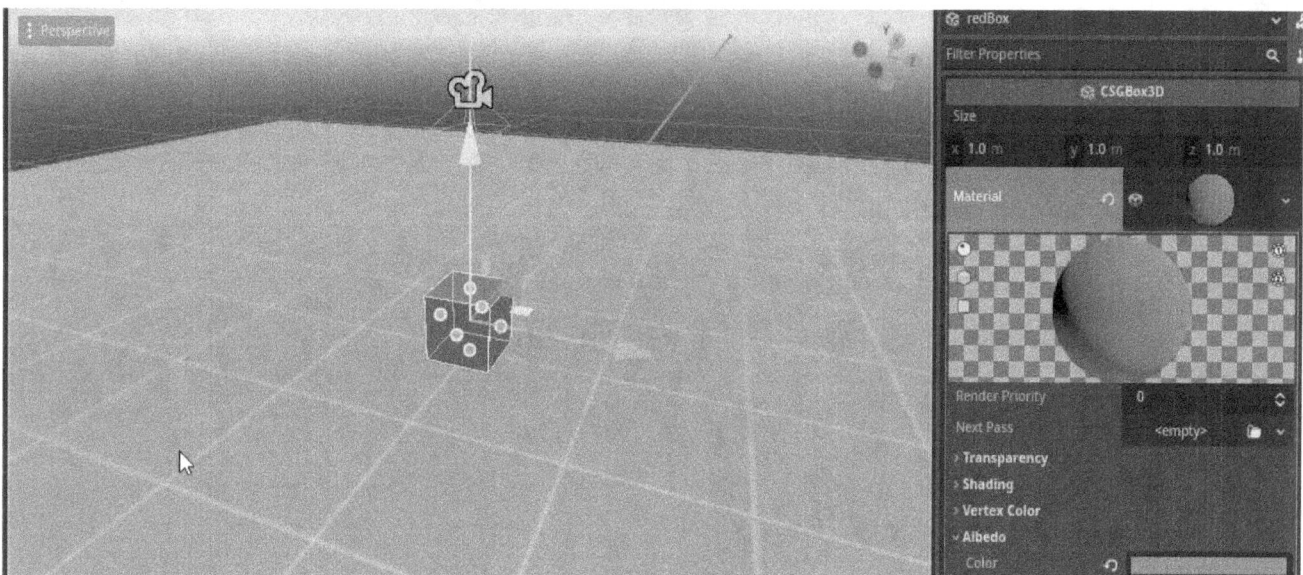

- If we zoom-in to look at the object labeled **redBox** in detail, we can see that the red color has been applied to all sides of the cube.

Now that we have created our first colored cube, we can create similar cubes using successive duplications to speed-up the process:

- In the **Scene Tree** window, select the object labeled **redBox**.

- Duplicate this object: we can right-click on this object and select **Duplicate** from the contextual menu or press *CTRL+D*.

- We can then rename the new cube (i.e., the duplicated object) **greenBox**, and move it along the **x-axis** (i.e., using the red handle).

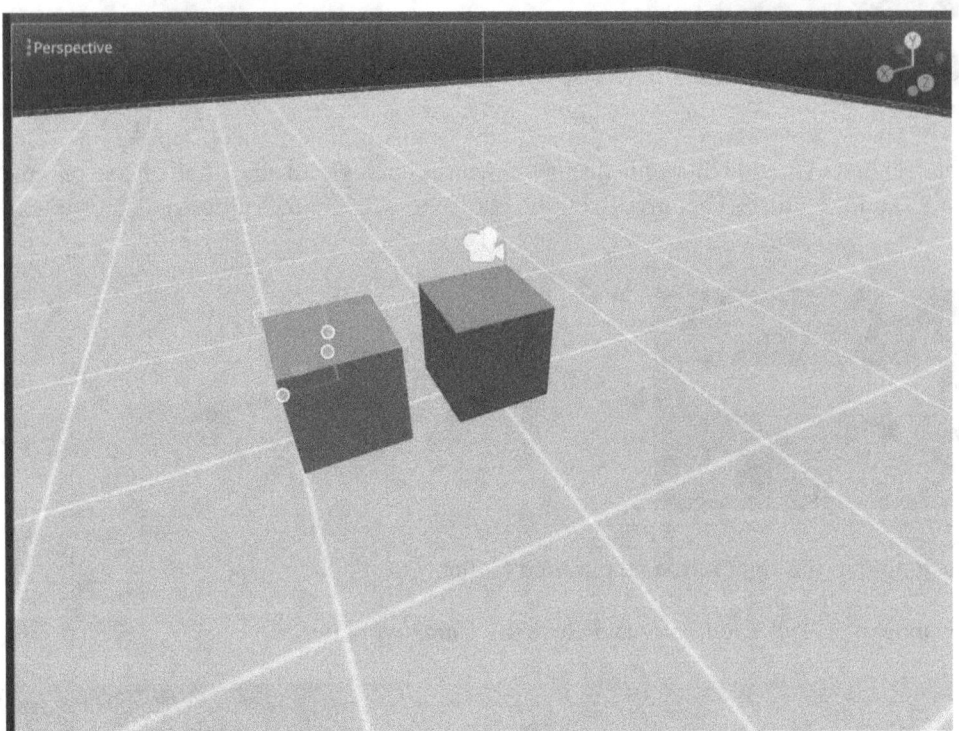

Adding a new cube using duplication

As for the previous section, we will create a new green color:

- Select the object called **greenBox** in the **Scene Tree**.

- Using the **Inspector**, locate the section called **CSGBox3D**.

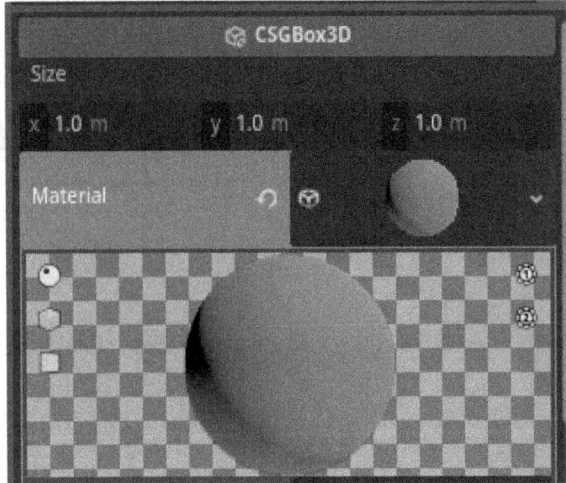

- You may notice that a red material is already allocated to this cube and this is normal since it has been duplicated from the red box.

- So at this stage, we just need to create a new material for this specific cube because we want it to be green (instead of red).

- Pleas click on the downward arrow to the right of the attribute called **Material**.

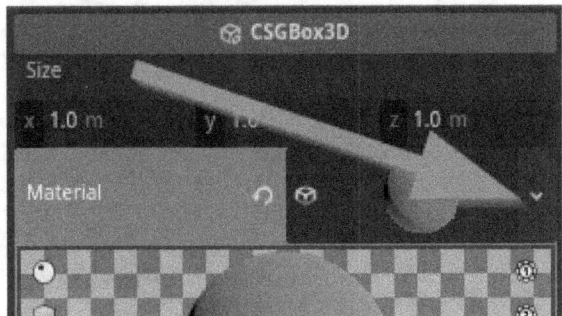

- From the contextual menu, select **StandardMaterial3D**; this means that we will create a new material that will be applied to a 3D object).

- You should now see a sphere, displayed in that section, as illustrated on the next figure.

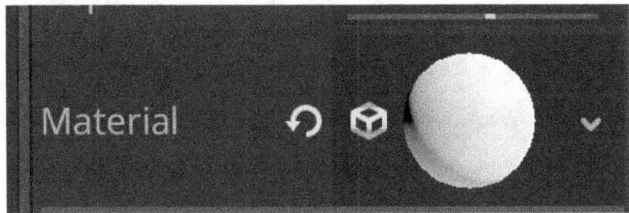

- Once you see this sphere, click on it, this should display a list of the properties for the material that you have created.

- Click on the parameter called **Albedo**, this will display a white rectangle to the right of the parameter along with an option to add a texture. This gives you the choice to select a new color or a texture for the ground.

- Click on the white rectangle to the right of the label called **Color**.

- As the color window appears, select a red green and close the **Color** window.

- You should now see that the green color has been applied to the second box.

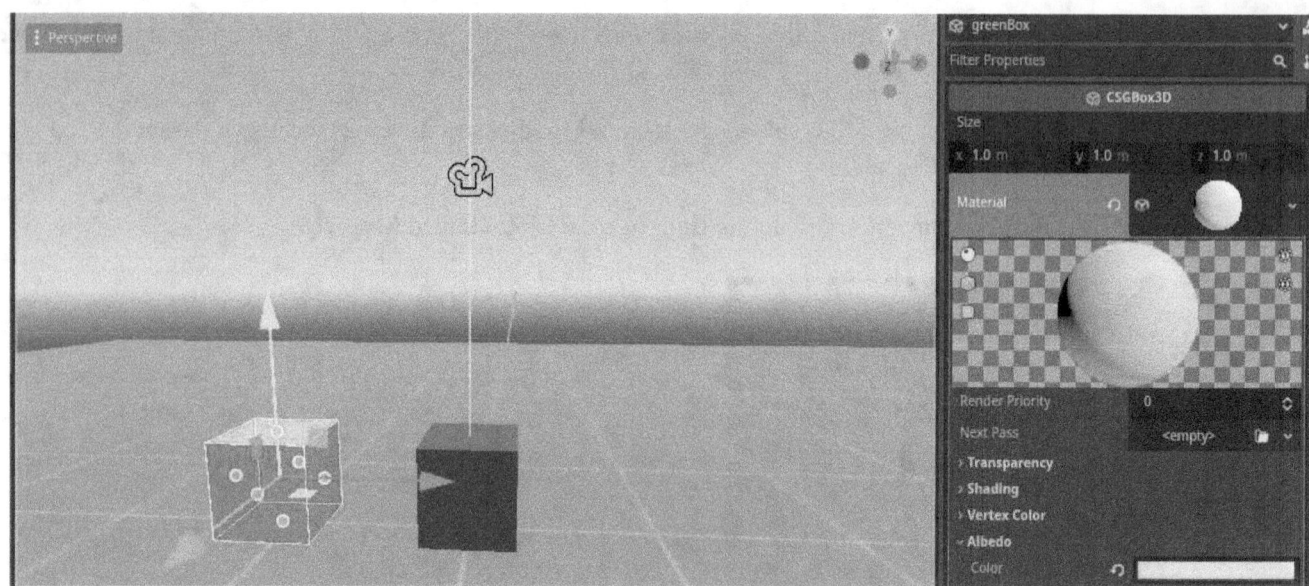

We can, again, duplicate this green cube (by default, it will be called **greenBox2**) and move this duplicate along the **x-axis**.

So at this stage we have three boxes using different colors; we can now try to see our scene through the camera's lenses so change the camera position to **(0, 10, 0)** and activate the preview mode by ticking the box to the left of the preview icon on the main view port; you should now see the scene from above.

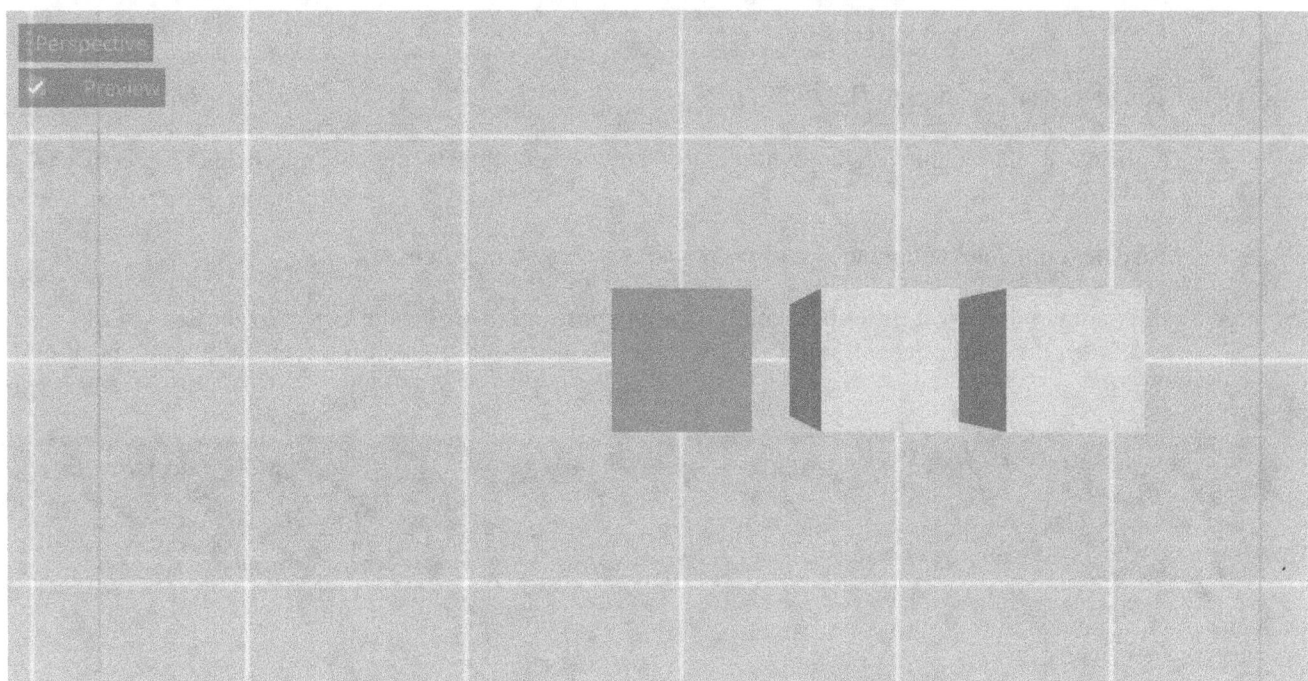

CREATING A SIMPLE STAIRCASE

As we have learnt how to create objects, there are a few shortcuts that we could learn to speed-up the process of creating a scene. To do so, we will go through a simple example of creating a staircase with boxes:

- Deactivate the **Preview** mode.

- Deactivate (hide) the objects **greenBox2** and **redBox** for the time being. To do so, you can select both objects and then click on the icon that looks like an open eye.

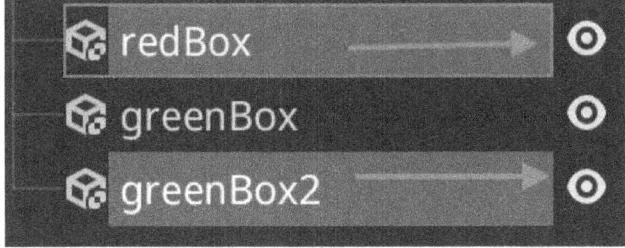

- After clicking on these icons, the objects should be hidden, and the eyes icons should now look like closed eyes.

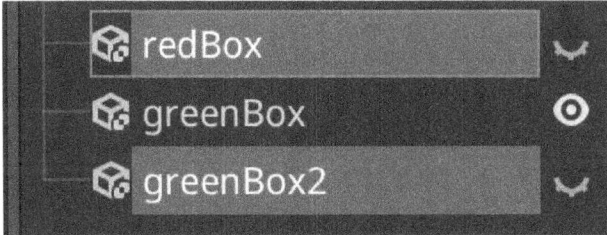

- Select the object labeled **greenBox**.

- Change its **scale** settings to **(1.5, 0.2, 1)**.

- Duplicate it three times. This will create three other objects named **greenBox3**, **greenBox4** and **greenBox5**.

- Move the duplicates along the **x-** and **y-axes** so that they form a staircase.

- For example, the object **greenBox** could be at the position **(3, 2, 0)**, the object **greenBox3** at the position **(6, 2.5, 0)**, the object **greenBox4** at the position **(9, 3, 0)**, and the object **greenBox5** at the position **(12, 3.5, 0)**.

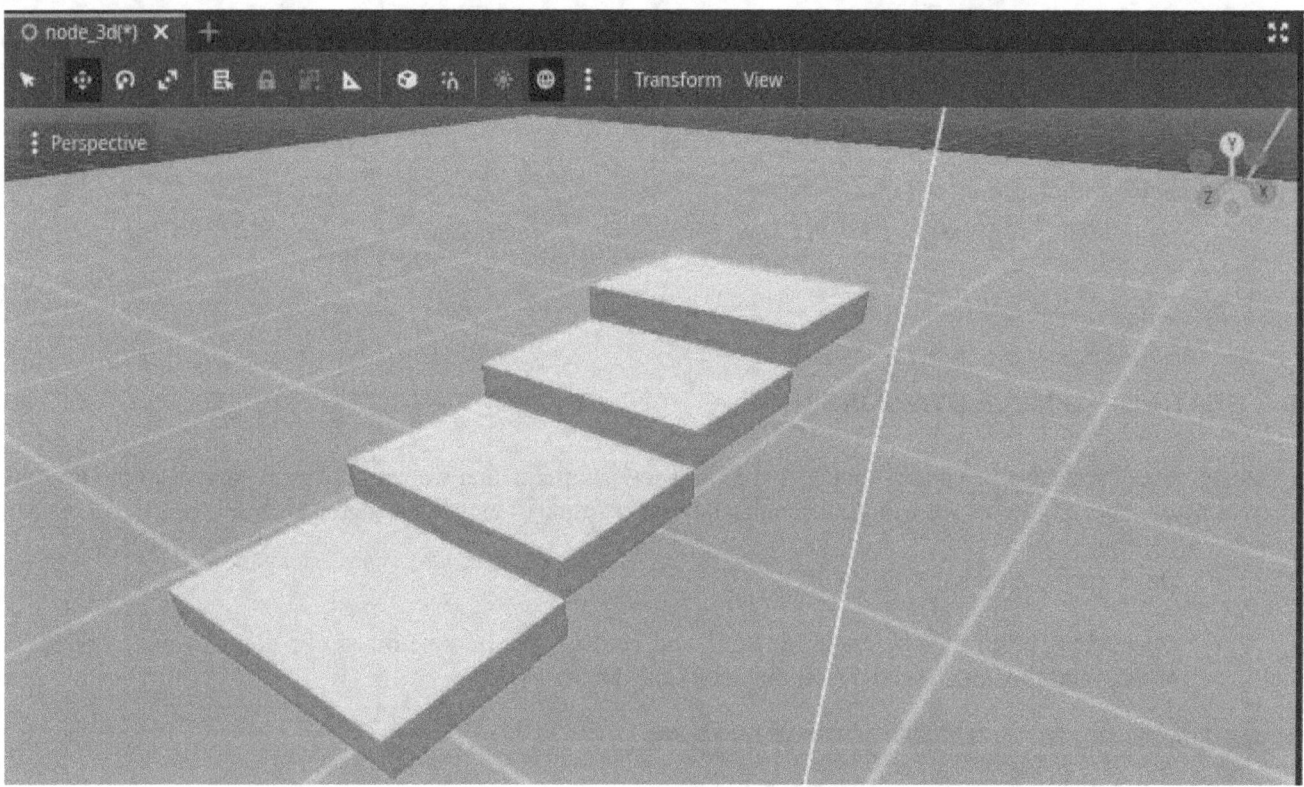

Managing and searching for assets and objects

As we have seen in the first sections of the book, it is possible to look for specific assets and objects in your project and in your scene using a search window and keywords. Let's experiment with these search features in the **Scene Tree**:

- If you look at the **Scene Tree**, you may notice a search window located in its top-left corner. It can be used to look for items in your scene based on their names.

- If we type the word **box** in this search field, it will list all the objects with a name that includes the word **box**, as illustrated in the next figure.

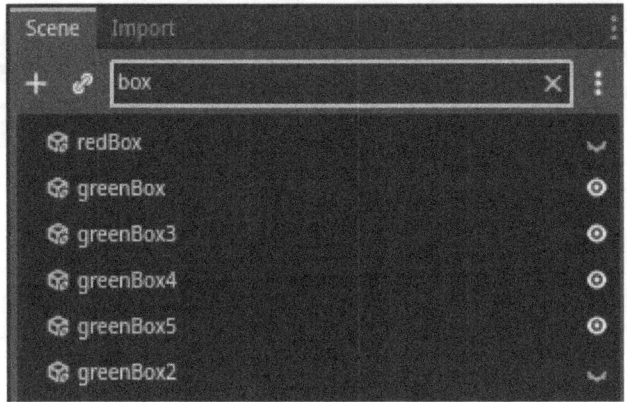

In a similar way, if we type the word **green** for example, it will list all the objects which names include the word **green**.

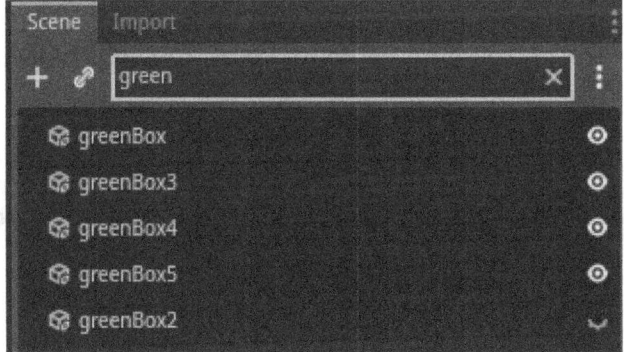

Let's see how we can perform searches in the **FileSystem** dock:

- If we select the **FileSystem** dock, you may notice a search window located in its top-left corner.

- After typing the word **tile**, Godot will show all the assets with a name that includes this word. In our case, it includes the texture that we have imported earlier (i.e., **tile.jpg**).

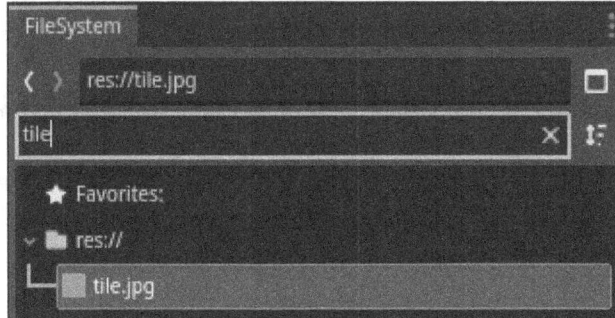

We can also perform searches in the **Inspector** tab, to look for a node's property:

- Select the node called **greenBox** in the **Scene Tree**.

- In the **Inspector** window, locate the search field and type the word **mat**.

- This will list the attribute for which the name includes the word **mat**; in our case, Godot is listing the attribute called **Material**.

Another interesting feature is the ability to group nodes. As it is, for example, we have built a staircase. However, we may need to move all the stairs as a whole, rather than moving each of these steps individually. In Godot, it is possible to group all of these steps by creating a parent node, which, in the **Scene Tree** view, is often used or referred to as a **Node3D Node** (for 3D scenes). Let's see how this can be done:

- Empty the search field in the **Scene Tree**.

- Right-click on the node called **Node3D Node** that is already in the scene and click on the option "**Add Child Node**".

- From the contextual window, type the text "**Node3D**" in the search field.

- Select the node called **Node3D** from the list.

- This will create a new child node called **Node3D**.

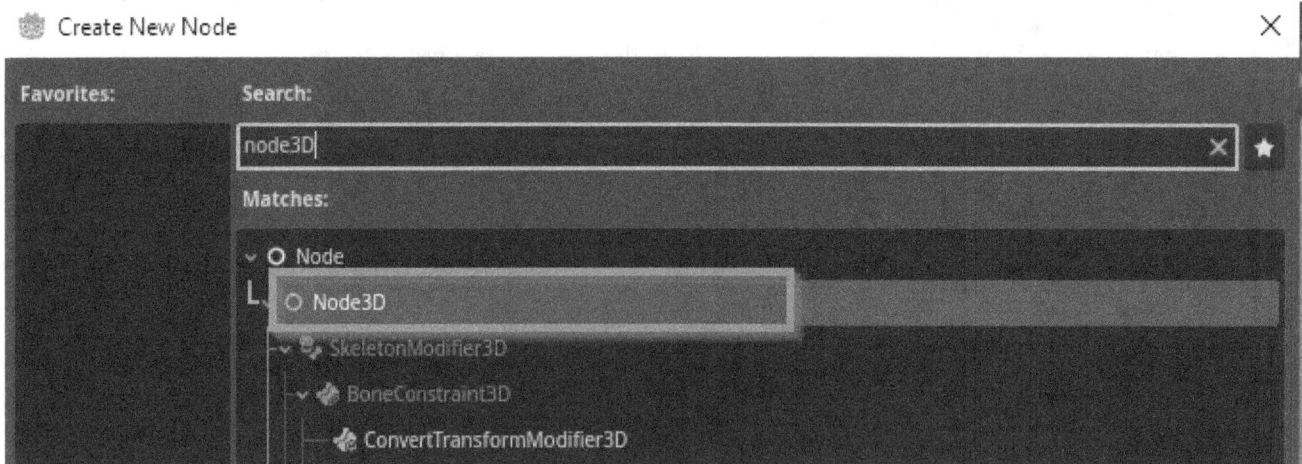

- Rename this object **container-parent.**

- Next, select the object called **greenBox** in the **Scene Tree**.

- Then press the **CTRL** key and click successively on all the other boxes that make-up the staircase, that is, the objects **greenBox3**, **greenBox4** and **greenBox5**.

- Make sure that the **container-parent** object is not selected and then drag all of the selected objects on the object **container-parent**.

- You should then see a downward arrow to the left of the object **container-parent** in the **Scene Tree** and all the previous objects should be listed under this object, as illustrated on the next figure.

Grouping objects

If we select the object **container-parent** in the **Hierarchy** view and if we use the **Move** tool, you should see that by moving this object, all its children are also moved accordingly.

SAVING THE SCENE

At this stage, we can save the scene:

- Select: **Scene | Save Scene As**.

- Choose a name for your scene, for example **scene1**.

- Press **Save**.

By default, the scenes are saved in the current project. You can see all the scenes included in your project by looking at the **FileSystem** dock or by using the search field in the same window.

BUILDING AND EXPORTING OUR SCENE

In this section, we will export our scene so that it can be visualized outside Godot. The process will involve importing the necessary Godot package to export our scene and configuring our **Export Settings**.

So let's get started:

- Select the menu **Project | Export**.

- In the new window, click on the button labelled **Add**.

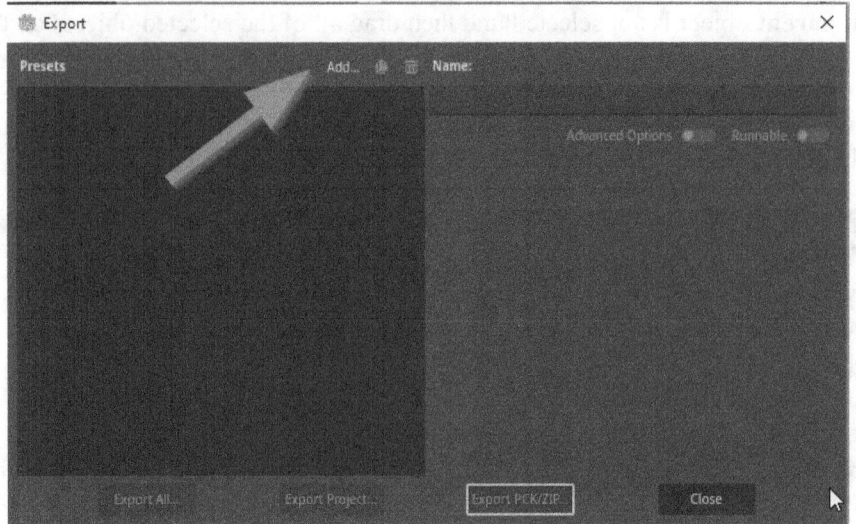

- This should display a list of possible platforms to export your game.

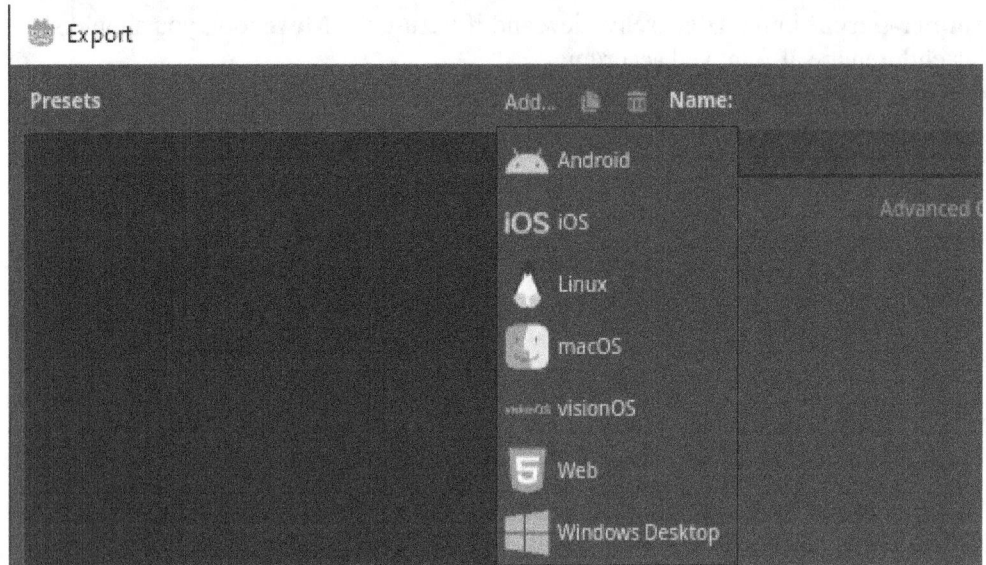

- If you have a Mac OS then select the option **Mac OSX** otherwise, use **Window Desktop** or **Linux/X11** depending on your operating system.

- In the new window, your platform should be displayed on the left-hand side, as illustrated in the next figure.

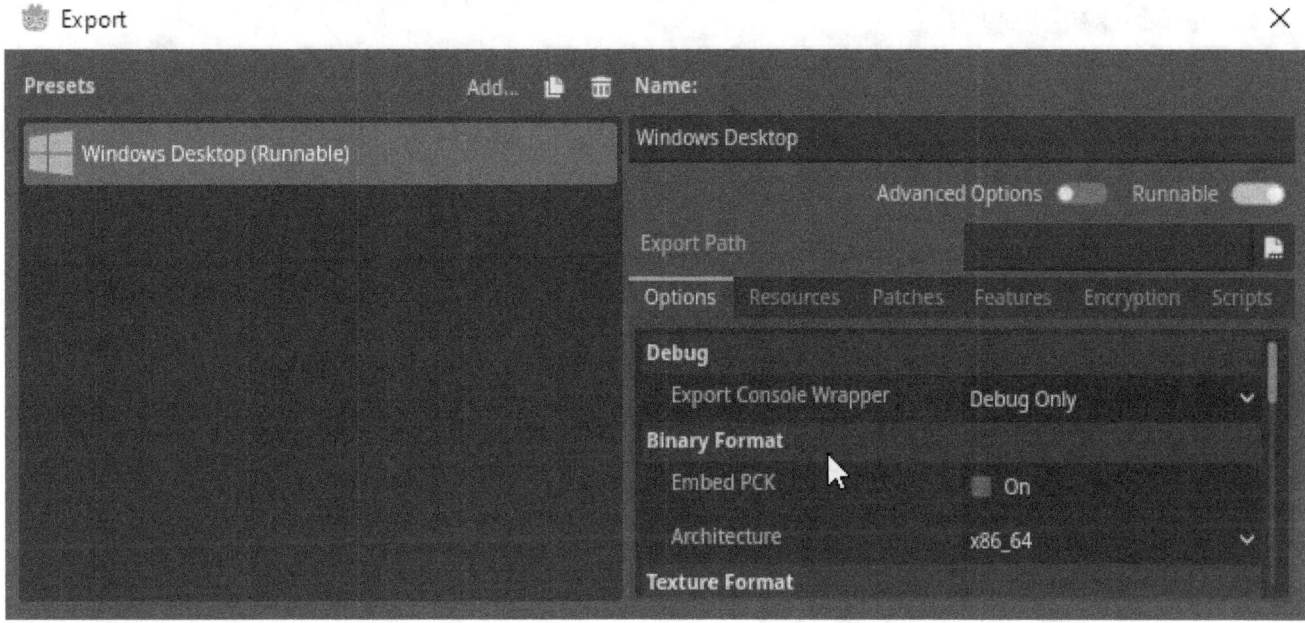

- You should also notice a message, at the bottom of the window, saying that you are missing export templates.

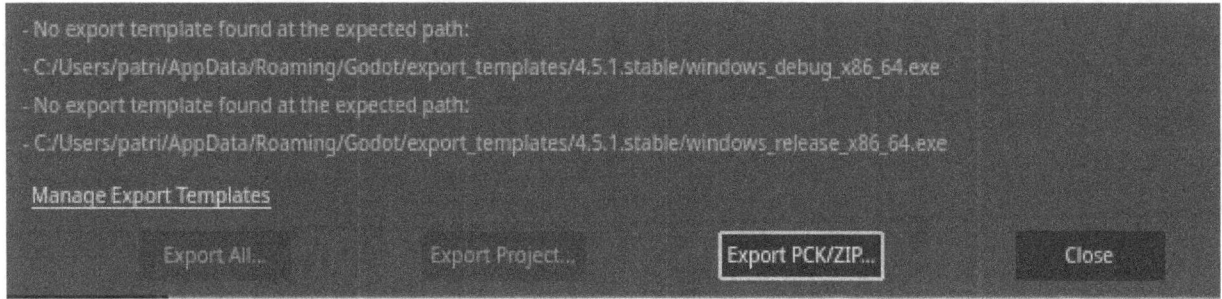

This message appears because Godot needs export templates to be installed before it can export your scene, and these can be installed using the following steps:

- Click on the link to the text "**Manage Export Templates**".

- This should open the **Export Template Manager**. You can also open this window by selecting **Editor | Manage Export Templates**.

- As illustrated in the next figure, Godot will let you know that you are missing a template for your current version.

- Click on the button labelled "**Download and Install**" to download and install the relevant template.

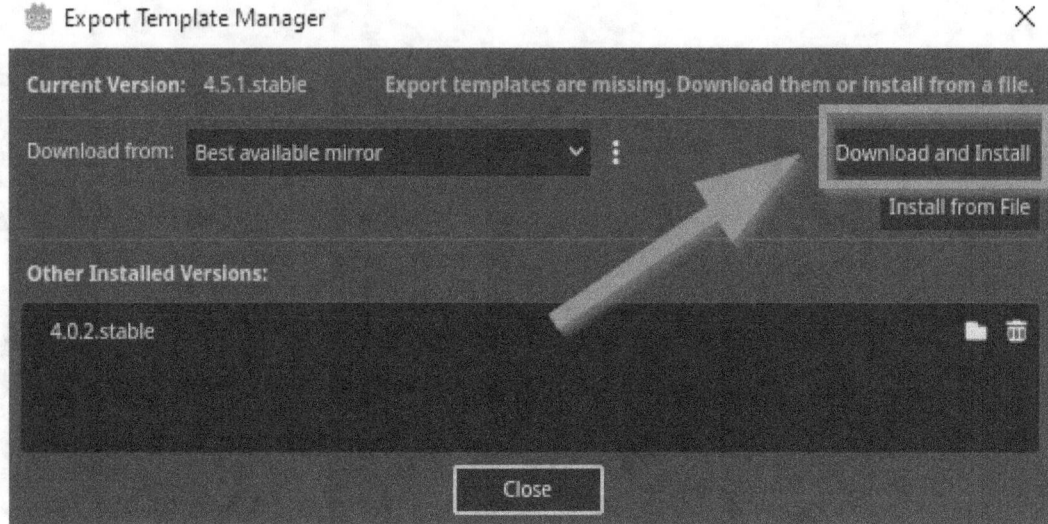

- The download will the start.

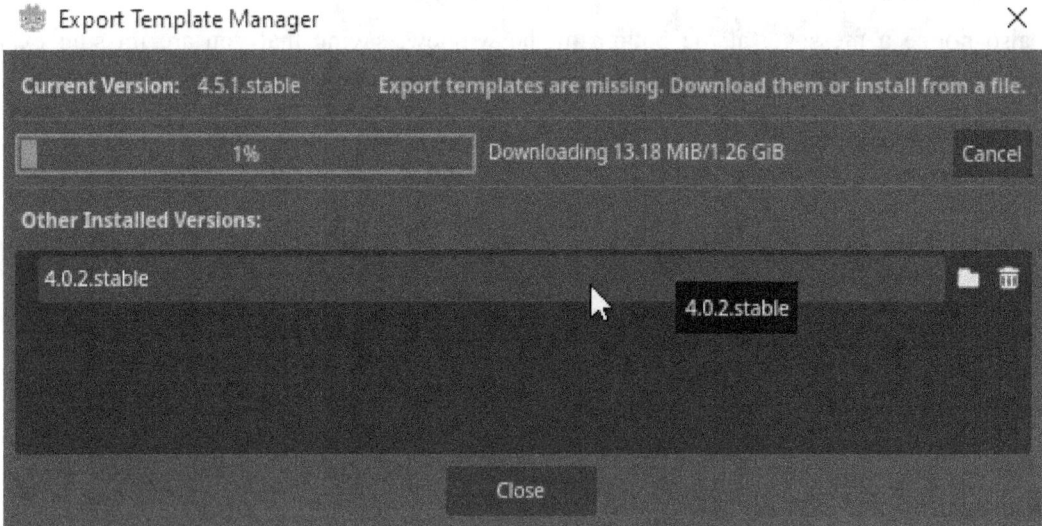

- This screen should be displayed after the download is complete

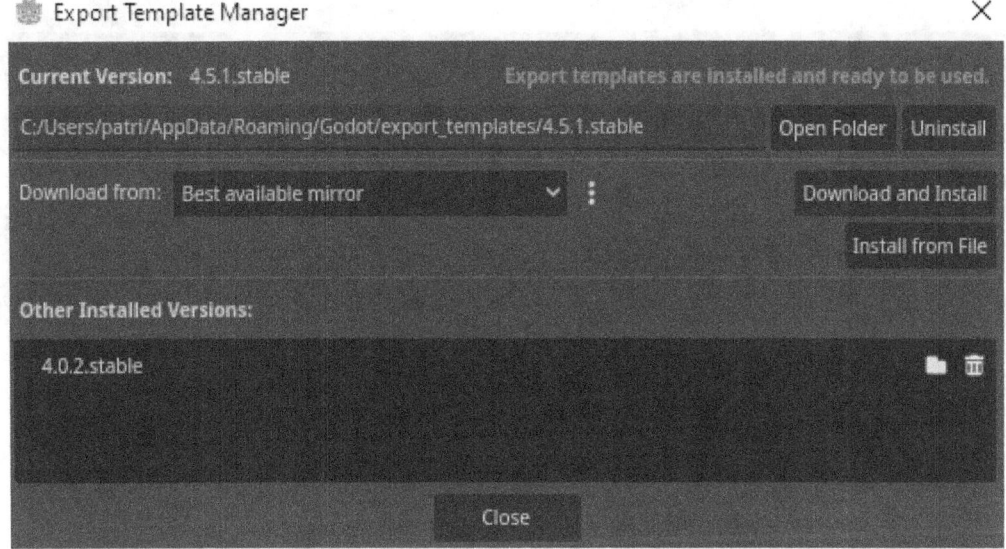

- You close the window.

Once this is done, we just need to do one more thing before we export our scene, that is, specifying which scene should be used for the exported game:

- Select: **Project | Project Settings**.

- In the tab called **General**, select the option called **Run**, and then click on the folder icon to the right of the label **Main Scene**.

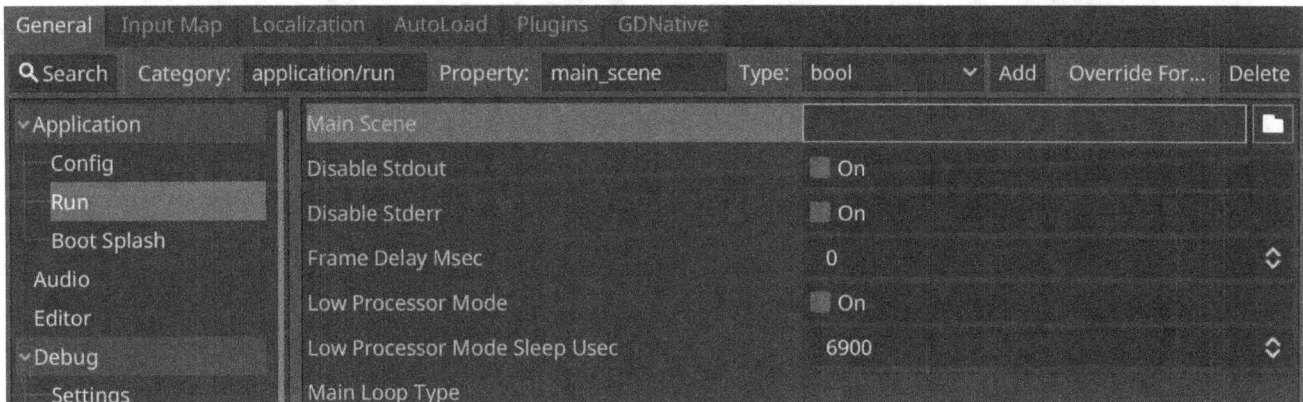

- In the new window, select the scene that you have just created (e.g., **scene1**) and then press **Open**.

- In the new window, **scene1** should now be listed as the **Main Scene** for the project.

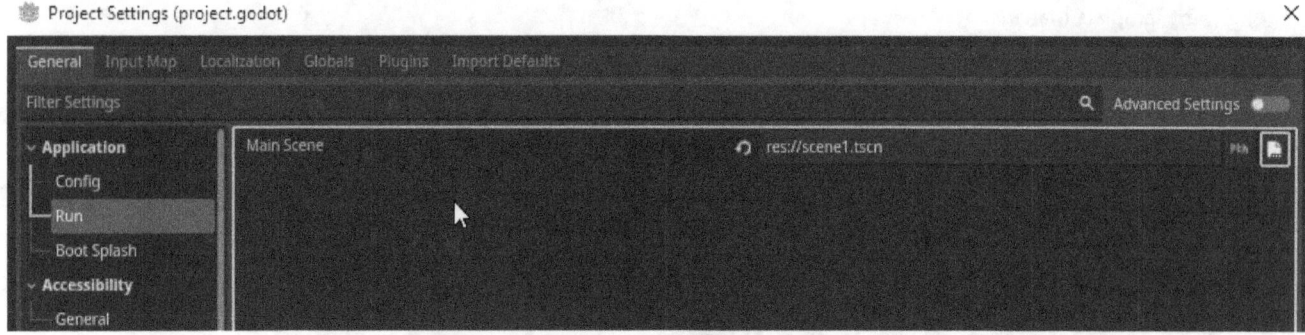

Once the main scene has been specified, we can now export our project.

- Select **Project | Export** from the main menu.

- When the window is open, select the option **Windows Desktop** from the left menu.

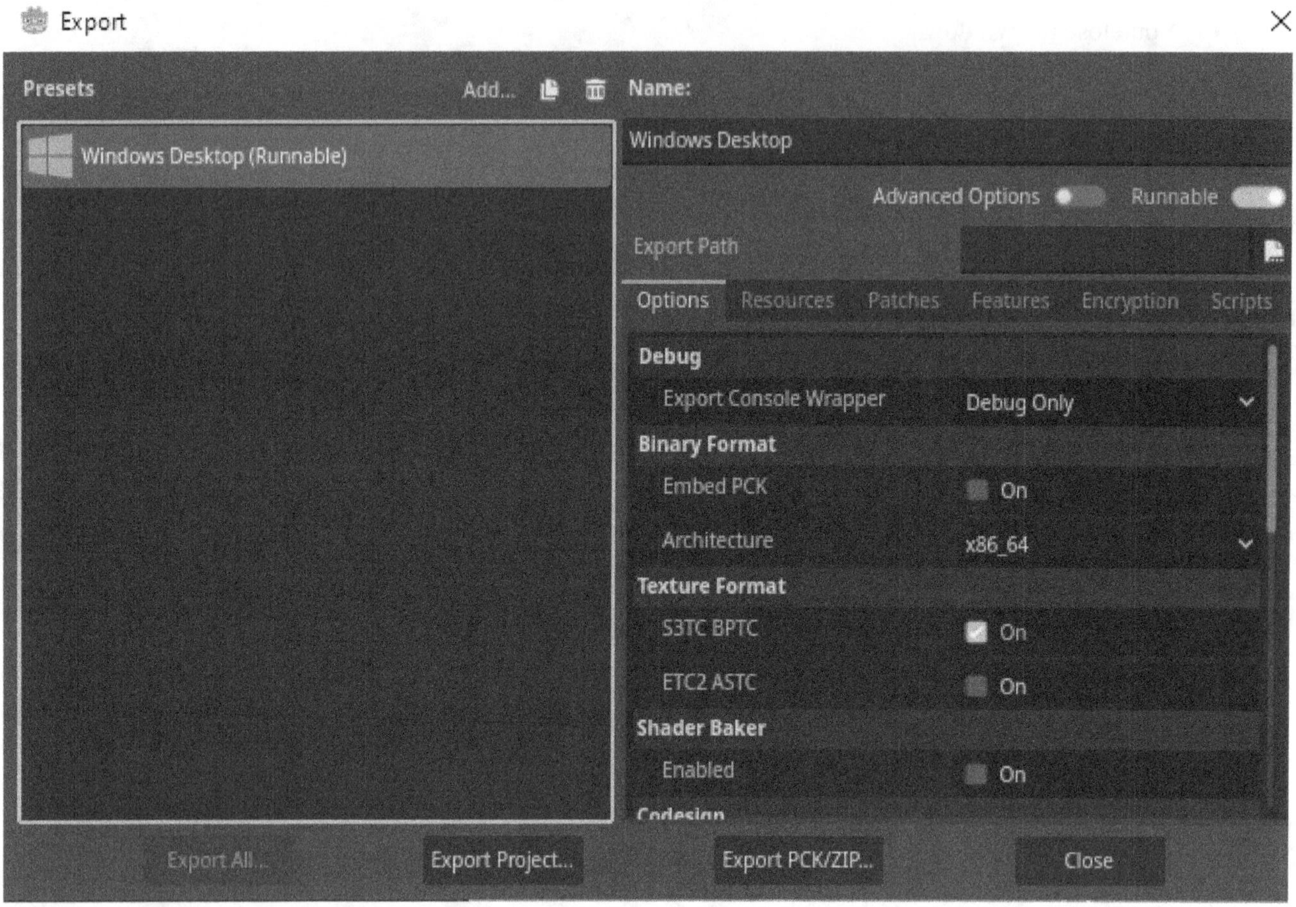

- In the new window, click on the button labelled **Export Project**.

- In the new window, give a name to your exported file, for example "**demo1.dmg**" and then click on "**Save**".

- Once the export is complete, and if you navigate to the folder that you have created for your exported game, you should see that it includes an executable file; in my case this file is **MyFirstProject.exe**.

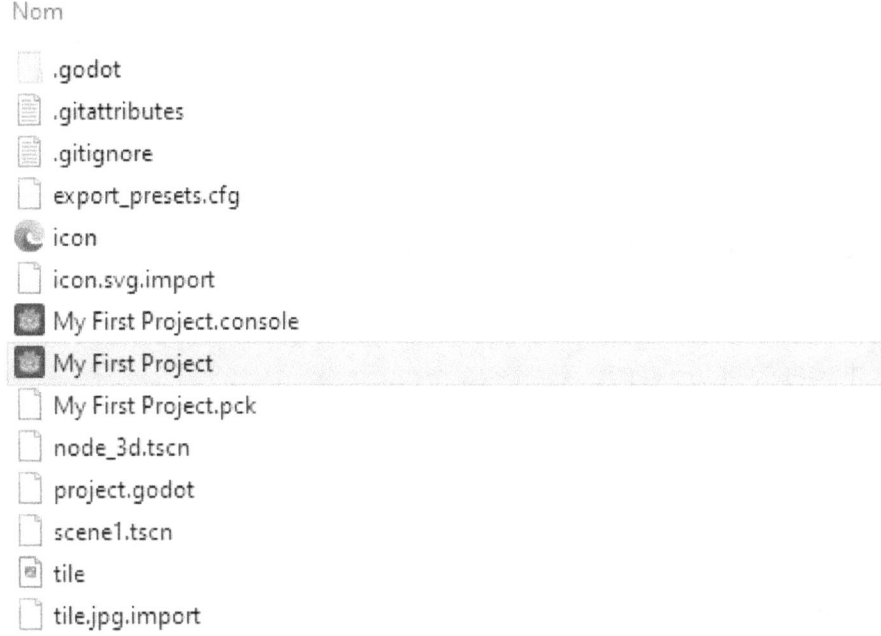

- Double-click on this file and check that the application opens; it should show the scene viewed from above.

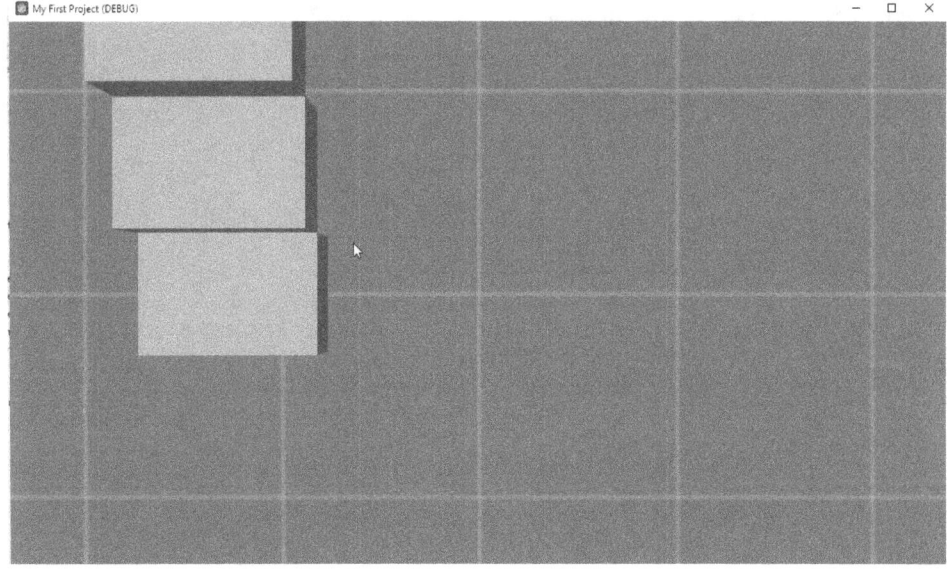

LEVEL ROUNDUP

SUMMARY

In this chapter, we have learned about several core features available in Godot. We became more comfortable with the interface and we learnt how and why to use the different views. We learned how to add and transform built-in assets, including cubes, lights, and cameras. We also looked into how to modify the appearances of each box by importing or creating materials. Building on this knowledge, we created a simple level with a staircase and a ground. We looked at different ways to manage the assets included in our project by grouping them (using Node3D Nodes) and by searching for them with corresponding search windows. Finally, we have learned how to export our scene as an executable.

Quiz

It is now time to test your knowledge. specify whether the following statements are TRUE or FALSE. The answers are available on the next page.

1. In Godot, all files and scenes are, by default, saved in the **FileSystem** dock.

2. All objects are usually represented as nodes.

3. It is possible to apply a texture or color to a cube.

4. The **RGB** code is used for colors.

5. The key *W* is the shortcut for the **Move** tool.

6. The key *E* is the shortcut for the **Scale** tool.

7. The key *R* is the shortcut for the **Rotate** tool.

8. It is possible to preview the scene when a camera has been added.

9. It is possible to preview the scene when no camera has been added.

10. A transformation applied to a Node3D node will also be applied to all its child nodes.

Solutions to the Quiz

1. TRUE.

2. TRUE.

3. TRUE.

4. TRUE.

5. TRUE.

6. TRUE.

7. TRUE.

8. TRUE.

9. FALSE.

10. TRUE.

Checklist

You can move to the next chapter if you can do the following:

- Add and combine built-in objects to your scene.

- Add a color or a texture to your objects.

- Manage and search for assets in your projects using relevant search windows.

- Group objects, and create a parent object, so that transformations are applied to all of the children (rather than individual transformations).

- Change the layout of your project's windows to suit your workflow.

Challenge 1

Now that you have managed to complete this chapter and that you have gathered interesting skills, let's put these to the test. This particular challenge will get you to become more comfortable with shortcuts.

Create a robot that does not have to be animated, as follows:

- Use built-in shapes (e.g., spheres, boxes, or cylinders).

- Combine these shapes to create the different parts of the robot.

- Group these shapes for the arms and legs, for example.

- Use duplication to speed-up your workflow (e.g., duplicate the left leg or the left arm).

Challenge 2

Create a scene that could be used for a platform game, as follows:

- Create a new scene.

- Add, move, and resize boxes.

- Add textures to these boxes.

- Test the scene.

CHAPTER 4: TRANSFORMING BUILT-IN OBJECTS TO CREATE AN INDOOR SCENE

This chapter helps you to create an indoor scene using basic shapes and textures. It will also show you how you can navigate this scene. Following the previous chapter, you will use your skills to modify objects (e.g., move, scale, rotate). You will also learn to configure lights, and textures.

After completing this section, you should be able to:

- Be more comfortable with manipulating and transforming objects.

- Understand how a texture can be tiled over an object.

- Configure the intensity of a light.

- Understand how to set up ambient lights.

THE PLAN

When you start creating a game, and although there are many resources available out there, you may just want to create a quick prototype to test the key features before you can (or hire someone who can) create a more polished level. Although you may have a 3D modeling background, many beginners who don't have this skill may need to be able to create their level quickly with basic shapes. This chapter will help you to do just that: to create a functional level with relatively simple shapes. For our first level, we will create a scene with the following features:

- An indoor maze with lights, textured walls, a ground, and a ceiling.

- Areas with lights.

- Dark areas where the player could be exposed or trapped.

To create this environment, we will be going through the following process:

- Use a template to create the maze (i.e., an image).

- Use this map to add objects to our scene.

- Remove this map.

- Add textures and colors to all objects in the scene.

Without a predefined map, it may be difficult to know where to add the different objects that will make up your scene. You can, of course, place the object based on a list of predefined coordinates. However, a map can help to visually and easily assess whether an object is at the right location. In our case, we will be texturing the floor with the map, then add objects on the floor, based on the outline of the maze, and then replace this outline with tiles, once all the objects have been added.

The layout of our level is illustrated on the next figure. It essentially consists of a succession of corridors.

As you can see, this is a rather simple black and white image that was created in *Photoshop*. It consists of a white background, which symbolizes empty spaces, and black rectangles of different sizes that symbolize walls. You can create a map of your choice very easily using other software such as *Paint* or *Gimp*. The idea of this map is to simplify the creation of the maze in Godot by specifying, even approximately, the location of the different parts of the maze. This way, we can follow our initial layout instead of guessing where to add objects. For the purpose of this chapter, this image was created using Photoshop. Its size is 100 by 100 pixels, and, if you are using *Photoshop*, you can also activate the grid lines every 5 pixels to obtain a subdivision every second pixel.

CREATING A SCENE AND IMPORTING THE NECESSARY ASSETS

Before we start to design this environment, we will create a new scene, and a corresponding folder where all the assets that we need will be stored. We will also import some of the textures required for this level.

First, let's create a new scene:

- Assuming that the project we have created in the previous chapter is open (otherwise, you can open it using **Project | Quit to Project List**), create a new scene (**Scene | New Scene**). Once this is done, you should have a blank scene with no nodes in the **Scene Tree**.

- Click on the button **3D scene**, in the **Scene** tab.

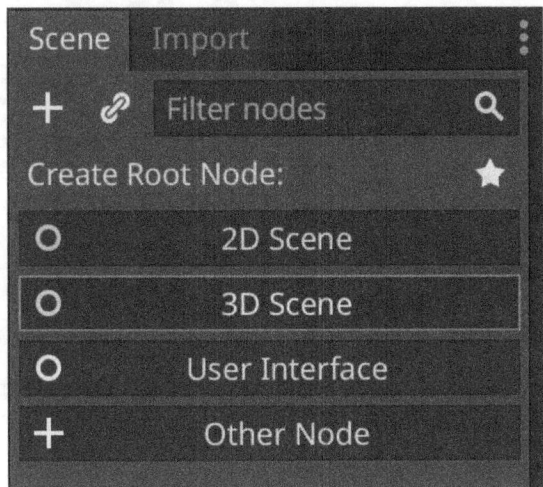

- This will create a new 3D scene with a root node called **Node3D**.

- You can save your scene, and name it **maze**, or any name of your choice.

We can now create a folder for our scene. While this is not compulsory, it helps to organize our project and to include and save all the relevant assets used for this scene in a dedicated folder.

- In the **FileSystem tab** window, right-click on the folder labelled **res://**, and then select **New Folder** from the contextual menu.

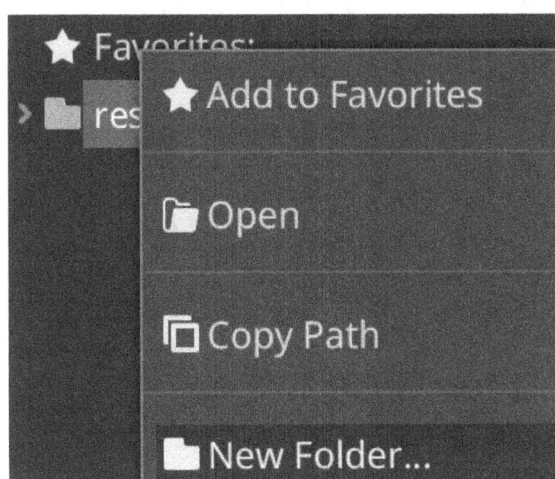

- When prompted to enter a name for the scene, name this folder "**maze**".

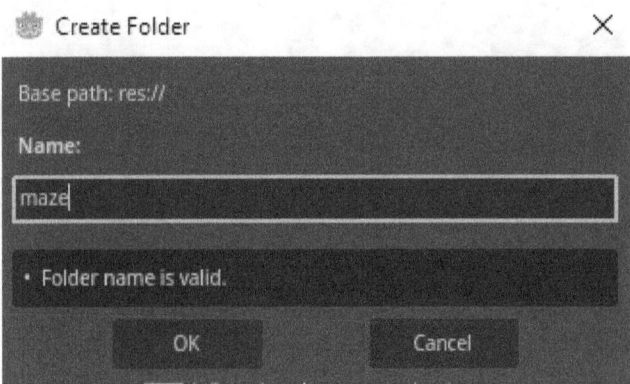

- Click on the button labelled **OK**.

- This will create a new folder labeled **maze** within the folder **res://**.

At this stage, you have already downloaded the resources for this book from the companion website. For this chapter we will need to import the images **bricks.jpg**, **ceiling.jpg**, and **gameMap.png**:

- click on the folder named **maze**, that you have created in **Godot**.

- Locate the folder that you have downloaded and unzipped from the companion website, in your file system.

- Drag-and-drop the images *bricks.jpg, ceiling.jpg, and gameMap.png* to the folder **maze** in Godot.

- These files should now appear within the folder called **maze**, as illustrated in the next figure.

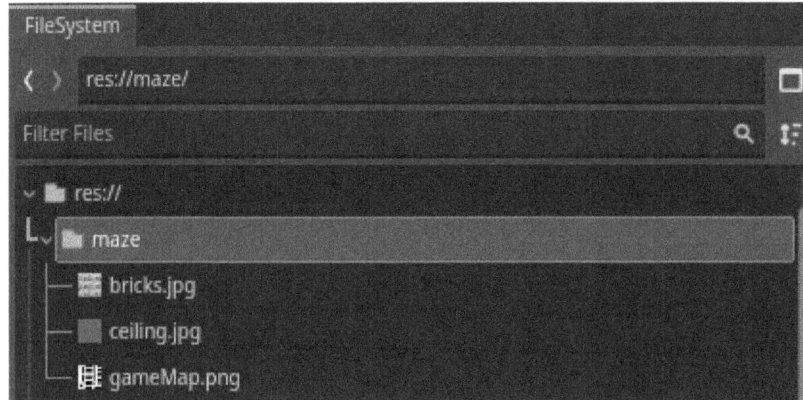

DEFINING THE OUTLINE OF THE MAZE

At this stage, we are ready to start creating our maze. First, we will create a cube that will be used for the ground and this cube will be associated to a **3D box**:

- Create a new **CSGBox3D** node: right-click on the **Node3D Node** already present in the scene, select the option "**Add Child Node**", type **CSGBox** in the **search** field, select the mode **CSGBox3D** and click "**Create**".

- This will create a new node called **CSGBox3D**.

- Rename this object **ground**.

- Using the **Inspector**, ensure that the position of this object is **(0, 0, 0)**.

- Unlock the "**Component Ratio**" attribute for the **scale** section.

- Using the **Inspector**, change the scale properties of this object to **(100, 1, 100)** so that it is scaled-up along the **x-** and **z-axes**.

- To make it easier to see the changes, we can look at the scene from the y-axis. This can be achieved, as previously, by using the **Gizmo** located in the top-right corner of the **ViewPort**, and by clicking on its **y-axis**.

- Using the **Inspector**, navigate to the section **CSGBox3D**.

- Click on the arrow to the right of the attribute called**Material**, and select the option **StandardMaterial3D** from the contextual menu.

- Click on the white sphere displayed in that section.

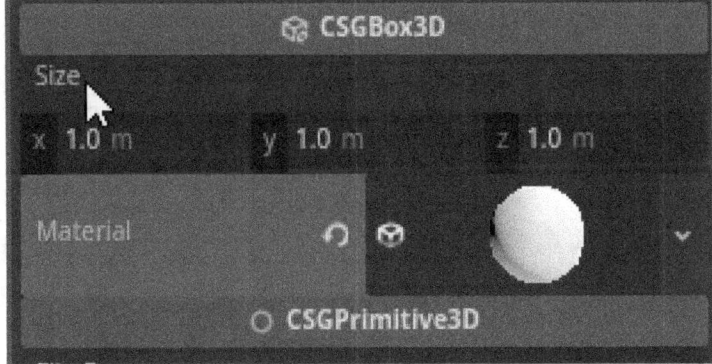

- This will list several attributes for the Material component.

- Select the option called **Albedo**.

At this stage, we want to specify a texture for the ground.

- Navigate to the folder that includes the texture that we have just imported, including the image for the ground, using the **FileSystem** tab (i.e., the folder **res:// | maze**). Once you have located this folder, as well as the texture that we need to use for the outline (i.e., the file **gameMap.png***), drag and drop this texture from the **FileSystem** window to the **empty** slot. This will, as we have seen in the previous section, apply the texture to the **ground** object, as illustrated in the next figure.

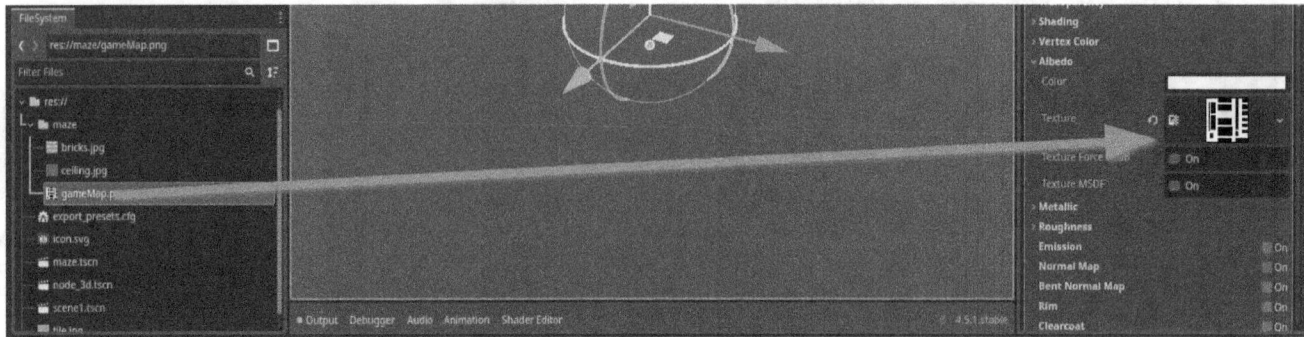

You should then see that the texture has been applied to the ground (**CSGBox**) as illustrated in the next figure.

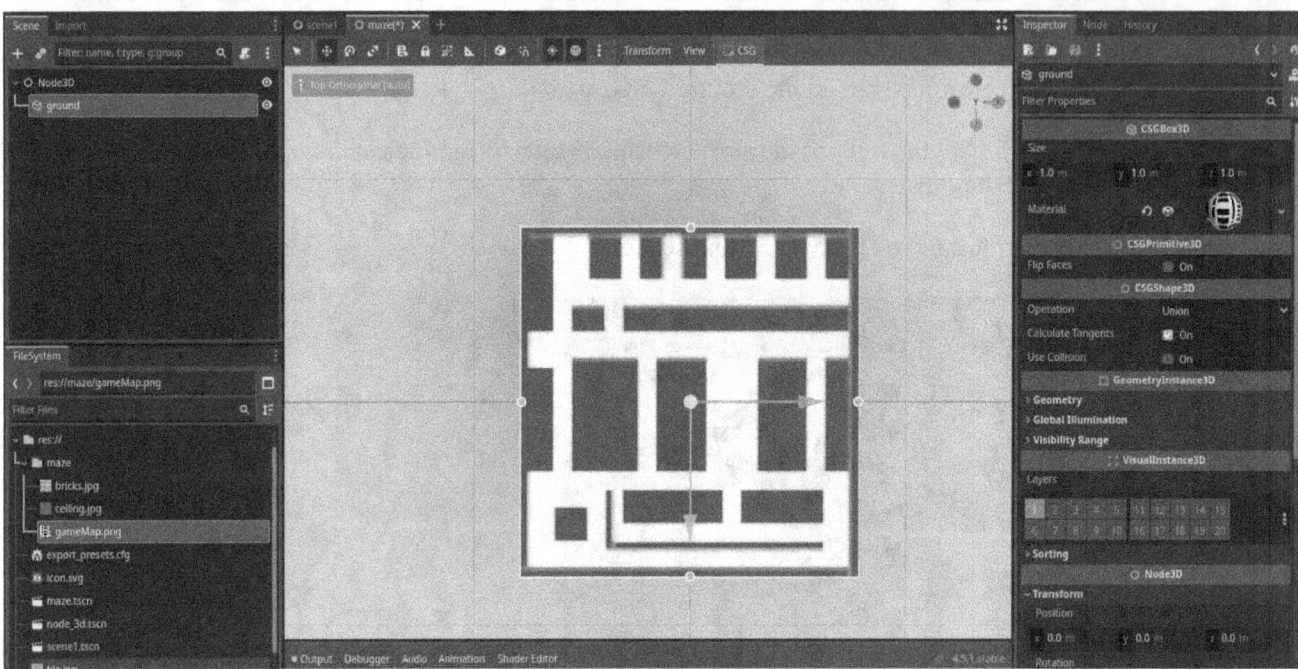

If, using the **Inspector** tab, we click on the attribute called **UV1**, you will see that the scaling properties are **(1, 1, 1)**, which means that the texture is tiled only once on all axes, and that's exactly what we need because the texture is supposed to represent the entire level.

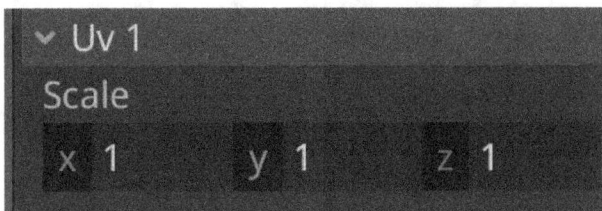

ADDING WALLS USING SIMPLE TRANSFORMATIONS

Now that the ground has been defined and that the template has been applied to the ground, it is time to create walls and other rooms, based on cubes.

- Create a new node of type **CSGBox3D** and rename it **room**: right-click on the node **Node3D**, select "**Add Child Node…**" and select **CSGBox3D**.

- Position this node (**room1**) just above the ground, for example at the position

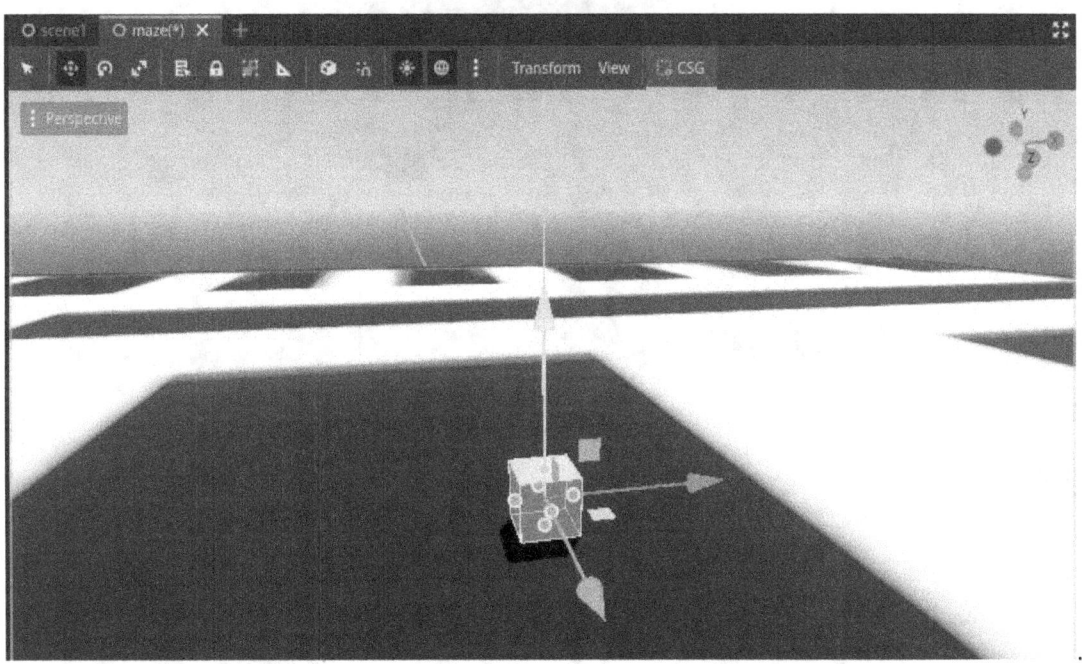

- Change its y scale attribute to **2.5** and adjust its **y** position so that it is above the ground.

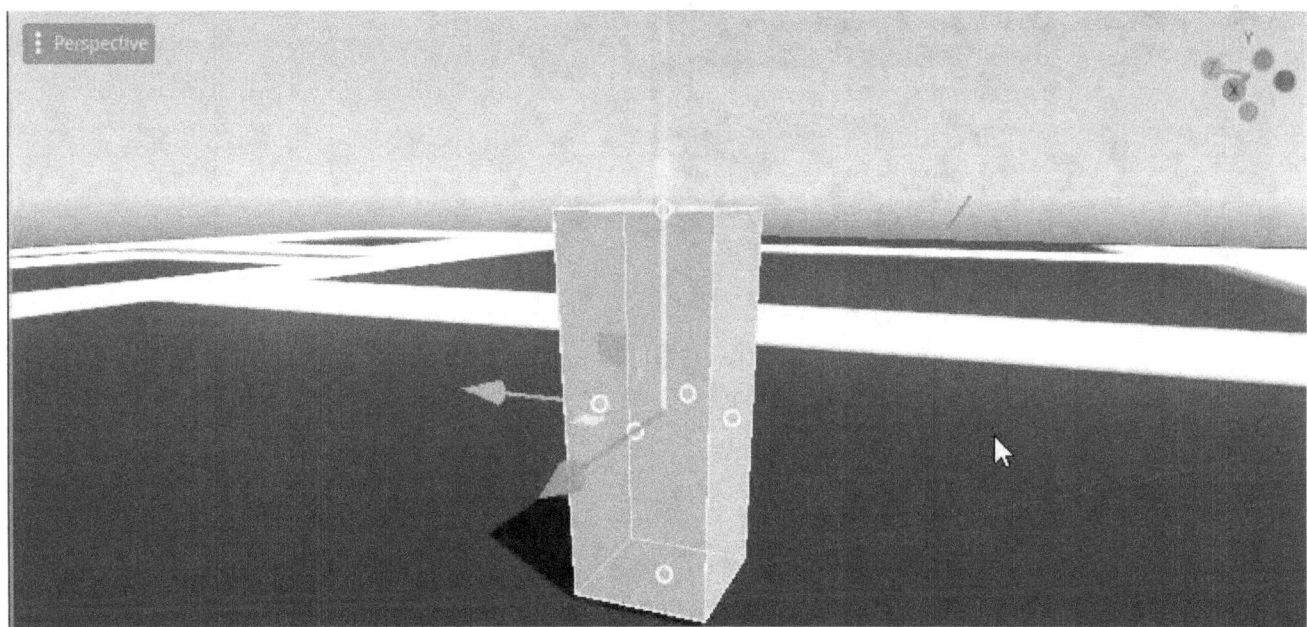

- Modify its shape or move it, along the x and z axes so that it matches one of the dark areas.

Once this is done, we can apply a texture to this room:

- Select the node called **CSGBox3D** that is a child of the object **room1**.

- Using the **Inspector**, in the **Material** section, click on the white sphere.

- In the next window, select the **Albedo** section and drag and drop the texture **bricks** located in the folder **res:// | maze**, to the empty slot in the **Inspector**.

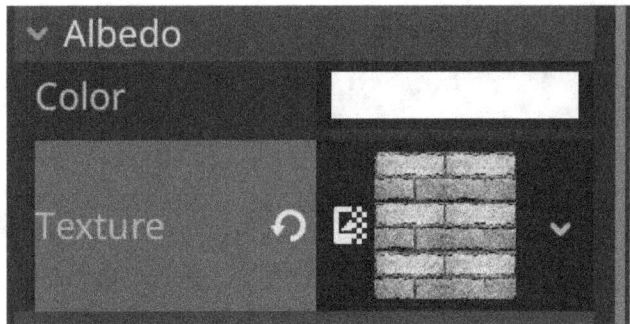

- We now need to change the tiling of this texture.

- Modify the **UV1** attribute in the **Inspector** to **(x=2, y=2, z = 1)**. This setting is arbitrary and you may use different scaling properties based on the texture that you have applied if you wish. To make sure that the tiling looks realistic, you may first zoom-in on the object, and then modify the tiling properties, so that you can observe and apply the **x, y** or **z scaling** values that work best for you.

- So that this box can collide with other objects, set the attribute **CSGShape3D | Use Collision** to **On**.

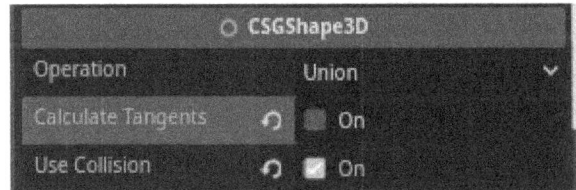

Once you are happy with the look of the room, we can duplicate this room and resize it to create another room:

- Duplicate the object **room1** in the **Scene Tree** view and call the duplicate object **room2**.

- Move the duplicate object near another black rectangle on the outline, and resize it so that it matches the area perfectly (i.e., at this stage, only the x and z **position** and **scale** attributes need to be modified). You can use the **Move** tool to move the new object, and the **Scale** tool to resize it.

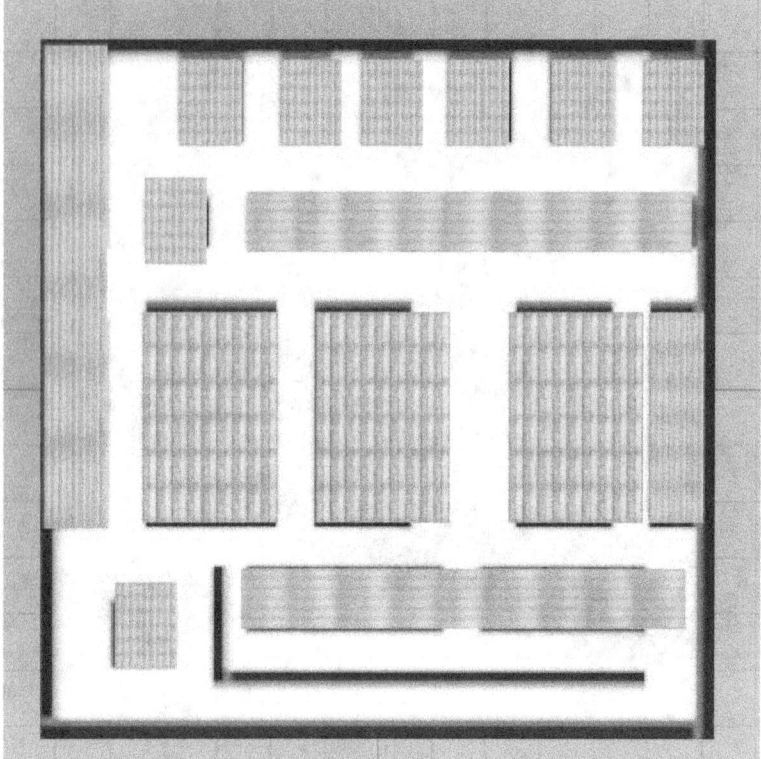

You can repeat this process to complete the entire maze.

CREATING THE EXTERNAL WALLS

Once you have created all the different rooms, the maze should look as described in the following figure.

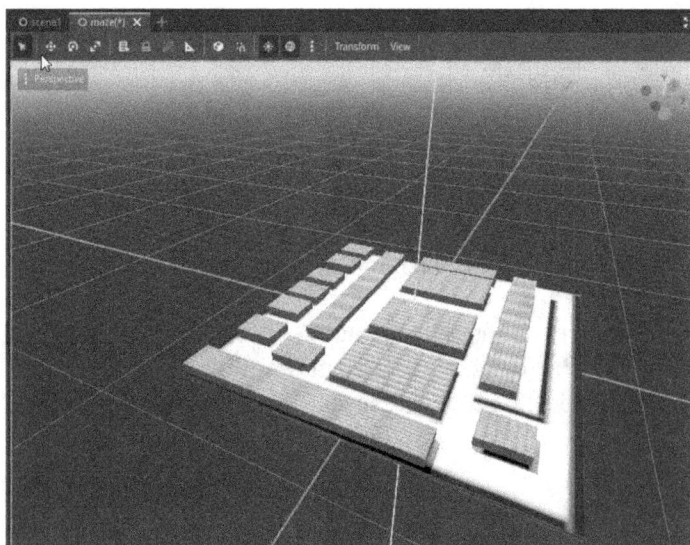

The maze almost completed (without external walls)

You may notice that the texture that we used for the rooms differs depending on the room it was applied to. This is because the tiling was based on the length of the initial room. We can leave this option as it is for now. However, if you wanted to improve the appearance of some of the rooms, you could define specific materials for each of them so that the tiling is set accordingly (since the tiling is linked to the material, a change in the **tiling** settings involves changing or creating a **StandardMaterial3D**).

So at this stage, our maze is almost complete, it only needs three more elements: four external walls, a roof, and some light. Let's create the external walls. To create the external walls, we can start by duplicating any of the existing rooms, and then resizing this duplicate. For example, we could, as illustrated in the next screenshots:

- Select and duplicate any of the existing rooms.

Note that if you copy/paste a wall, make sure it is pasted atop the root node (Node3D)

- Rename this duplicate **northWall**.

- Change its size to (1,1,1)

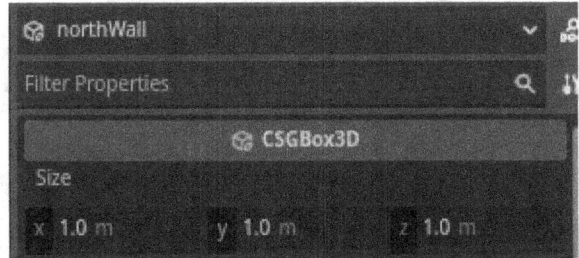

- Change its scale property to **(1, 2.5, 100)** and its position property to **(-50, 2.5, 0)**.

As you can see, the process is rather easy, and we can repeat it to create the three other external walls:

- Duplicate the node **northWall** and rename it **southWall**.

- Change its transform property to **(50, 2.5, 0)**.

- Duplicate the node **northWall** and rename it **westWall**.

- Change its transform property to **(0, 2.5, 50)** and its rotation property to **(0, 90, 0)**.

- Finally, Duplicate the node **westWall** and rename it **eastWall**.

- Change its transform property to **(0, 2.5, -50)**.

ADDING A FIRST-PERSON CONTROLLER TO NAVIGATE THROUGH THE SCENE

At this stage, we have managed to create the floor, several rooms, and the external walls for our maze, and it would be great to be able to navigate through the maze. To do so, we will add **Character Controller** to the scene so that we can walk through the maze and see how it will appear to the player. So let's do the following:

- Open the **AssetLib** window (top workspace).

- Enter the text "**First person Controller**" in the search field.

- Double-click on the result labelled "**Simple First Person Controller**".

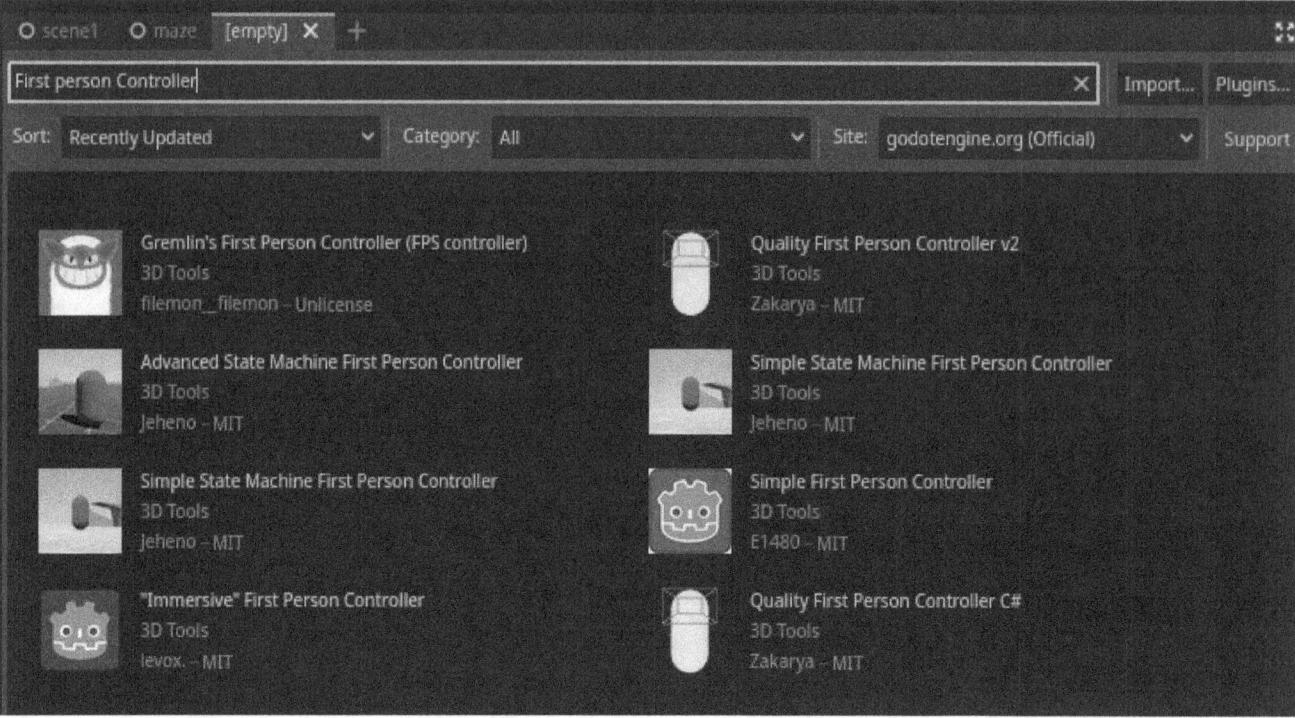

- In the new window, click on **Download**.

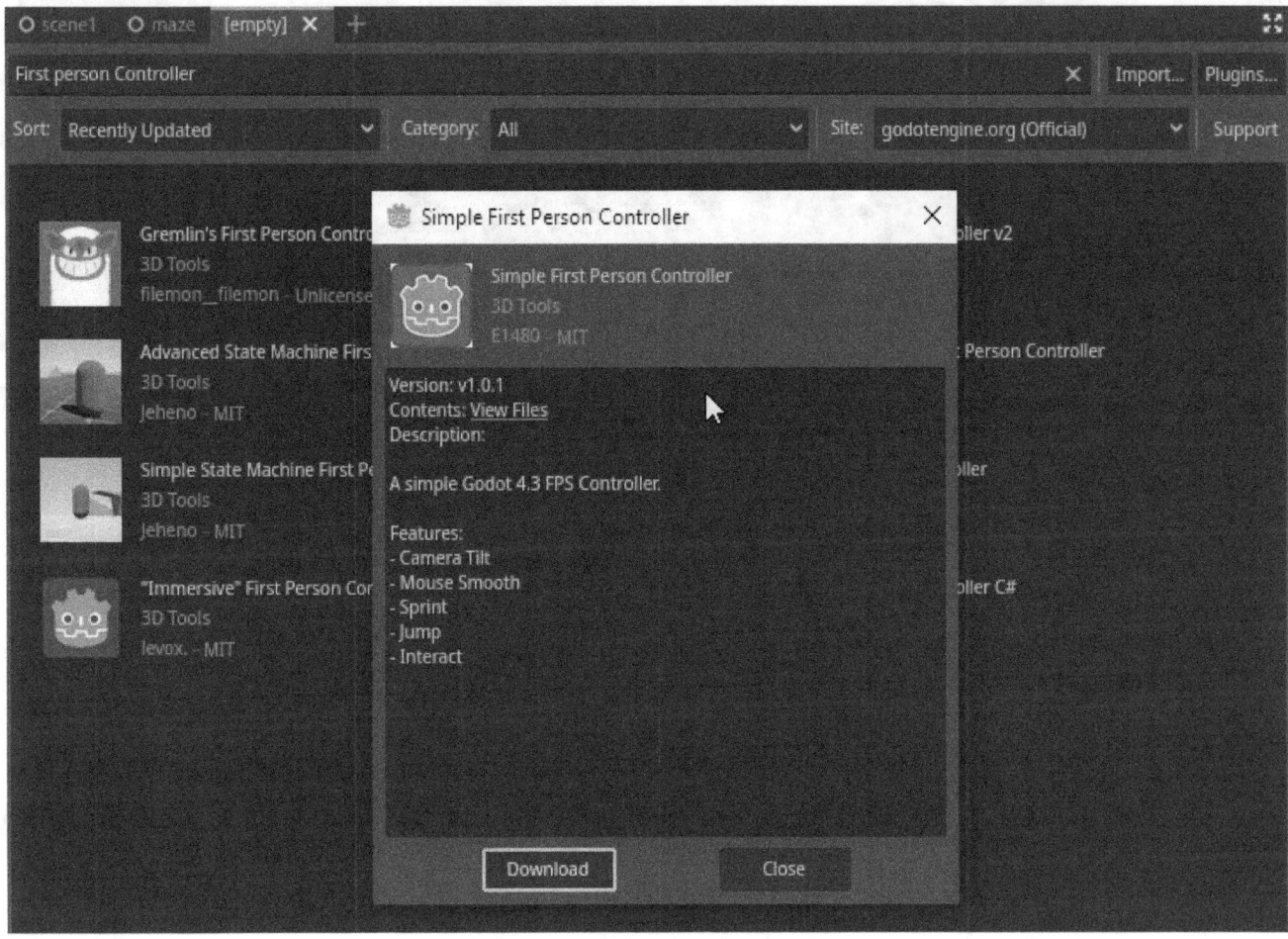

- Then, click on **Install**.

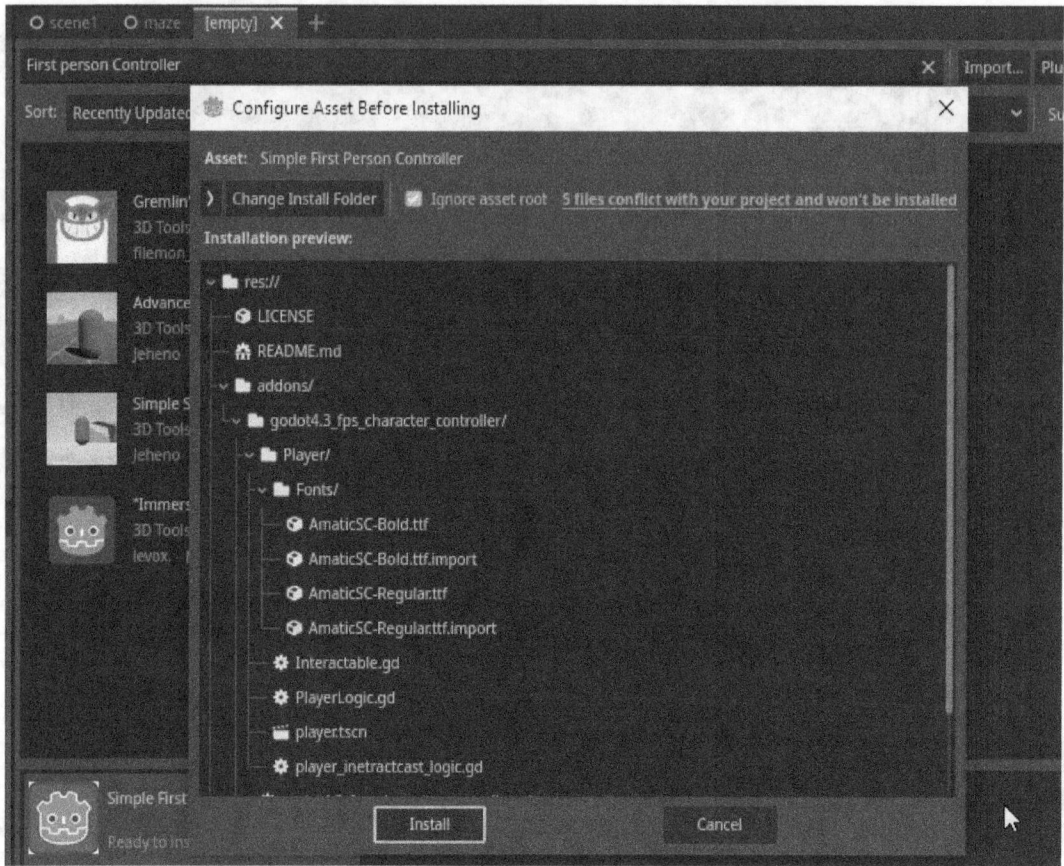

- After a few seconds Godot will let you know that the package has been downloaded successfully.

- Looking at the **FileSystem** dock, **you** should now see a folder called **player** (i.e., **res://assests/player**) and within this folder, an asset called **Player.tscn**.

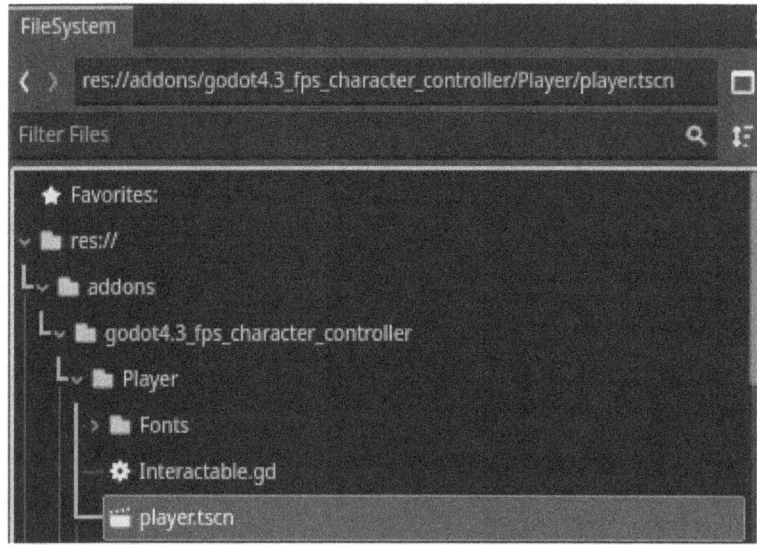

- You can now drag and drop this file (**Player.tscn**) on the node called **Node3D**, in the **SceneTree** dock; this will create a node called **Player** that is a child of the node called **Node3D**.

- Using the **Move** tool, you can move this node so that it not inside a wall; also ensure that the y coordinate is **1**.

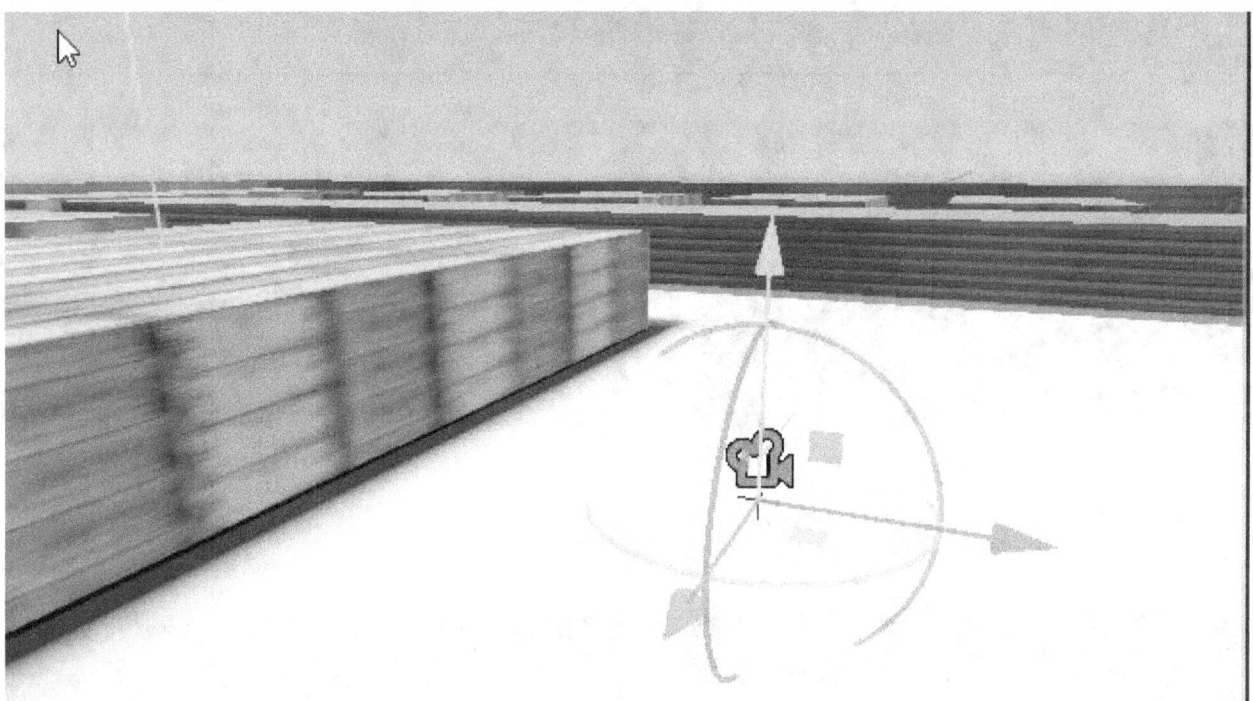

Before we can use this controller, we just need to set the current scene as the default one and to also reassign the keyboard keys to the movement:

- Select the object called **ground** and make sure that its attribute "**Use Collision**" is set to **True**.

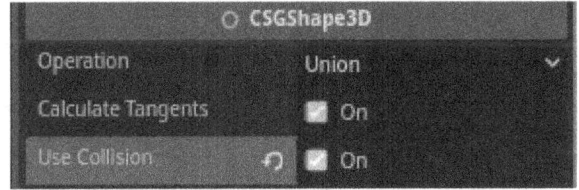

- From the top menu, select: **Project | Project Settings | General | Application | Run**.

- Click on the button to the right of the attribute "**Main Scene**", to select the scene maze from the File System

- Change the main scene to the **maze** scene and press "**Close**" to close that window.

- From the top menu, select: **Project | Project Settings | Input Map**

- In the new window, enter the text "**Forward**" in the top field and then press the button labelled **Add** (to the right of your screen).

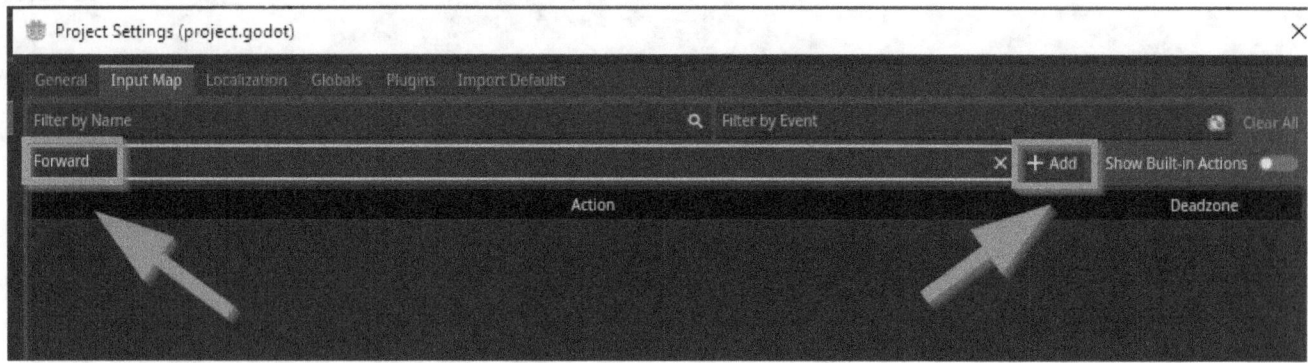

- Once the key has been added, click on the + button to the right of the key and select "**Key**" from the contextual menu, as per the next figure.

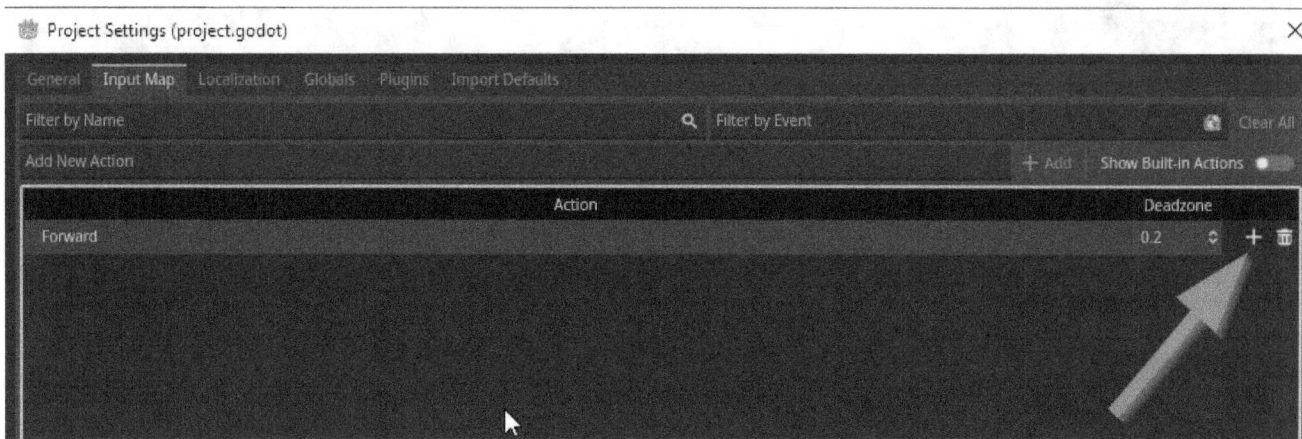

- Press the **Up Arrow** on your keyboard and then press **OK**.

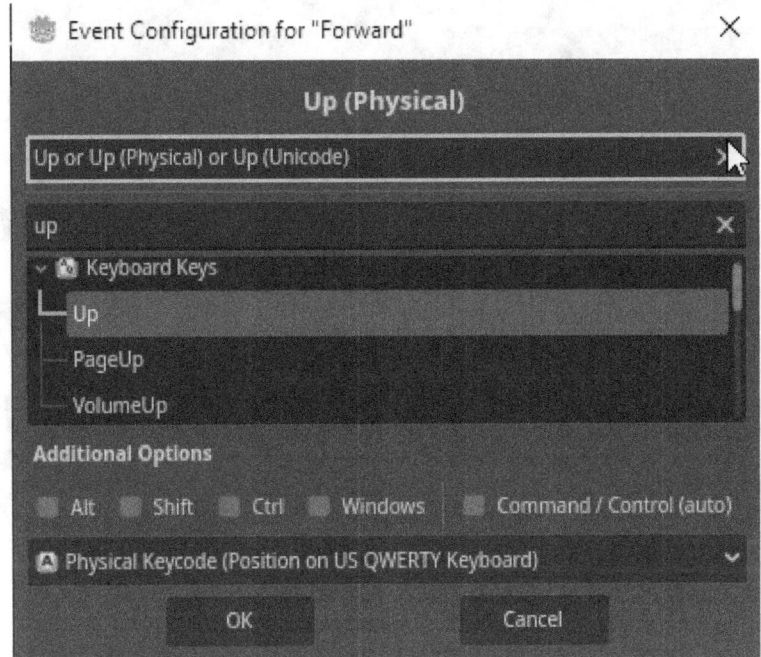

repeat the previous steps to add the following settings:

- **Backward** using the **Down Arrow**.

- **Jump** using the **Space Bar**.

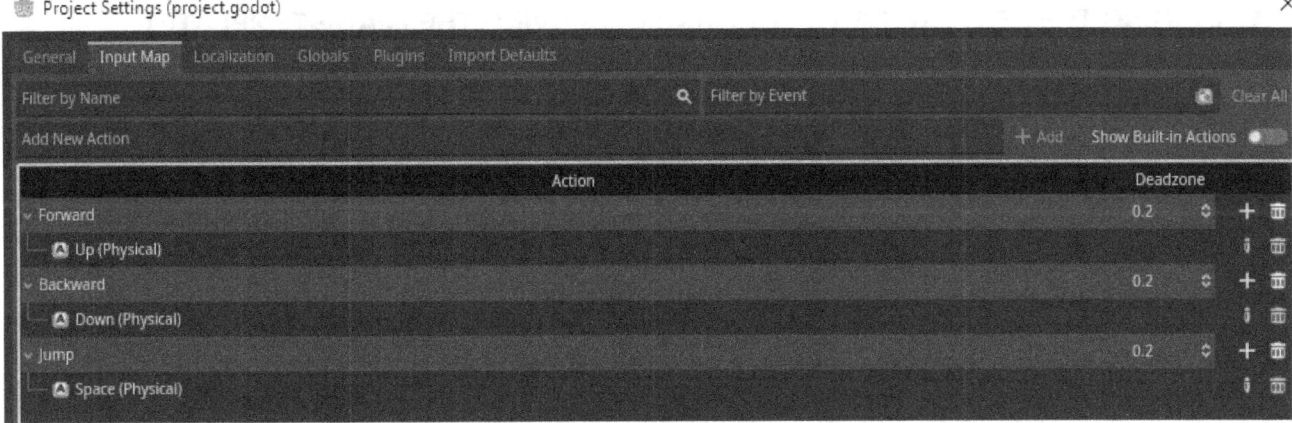

At this stage, you can test the scene by pressing **F5** (this is to play the scene; you can also press the corresponding button in the top-right corner - the fourth from the left), and you should be able to navigate the scene without going through the walls by pressing the arrow keys on your keyboard and the mouse to navigate. You can stop playing the scene at any stage using F8.

CHANGING THE TEXTURE OF THE GROUND (REMOVING THE IMAGE TEMPLATE)

At this stage, our level is pretty much ready to be viewed, except for the ground. If you remember, the texture used for the ground has been, until now, a template with white and black boxes that indicated where to add the cubes that defined the rooms. Because we have completed the layout for the maze, we don't need this texture anymore. We can, instead, use a more realistic texture for the ground, such as the **tile** texture that we had initially applied to the ground in the previous chapter. So let's make this change:

- In the **SceneTree** tab, locate the object labeled **ground.**

- In the Inspector, locate the section called **CSGBox3D**, and click on the textured sphere to the right of the label called **Material**.

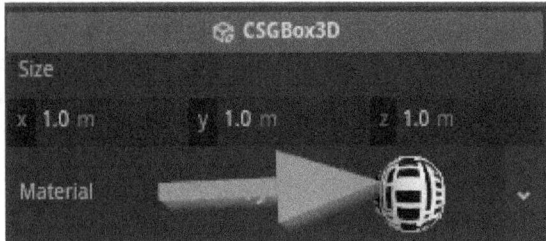

- After clicking on this icon, a new window will appear with a list of attributes; expand the attribute called **Albedo**, by clicking on the arrow to the left of the label **Albedo**.

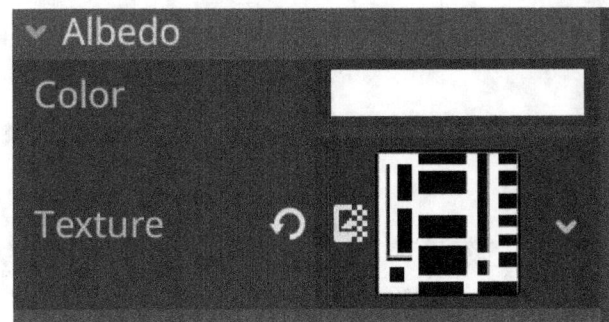

- We can now replace the current texture by dragging and dropping the texture called **tile.jpg** from the **FileSystem** tab to the attribute called **Texture**.

As soon as you have dropped the texture, you will see that the ground has changed color and is now featuring the texture **tile.jpg**; however, at this stage we also need to modify the way the texture is repeated over the surface (i.e., the **tiling**), and this will be done through the attribute called **UV1**.

- Select the attribute called **UV1** for the current texture, and change the scaling properties to **(20, 20, 20)** as illustrated in the next figure.

- As you make these changes, you will see that the tile texture is repeated more frequently over the ground surface.

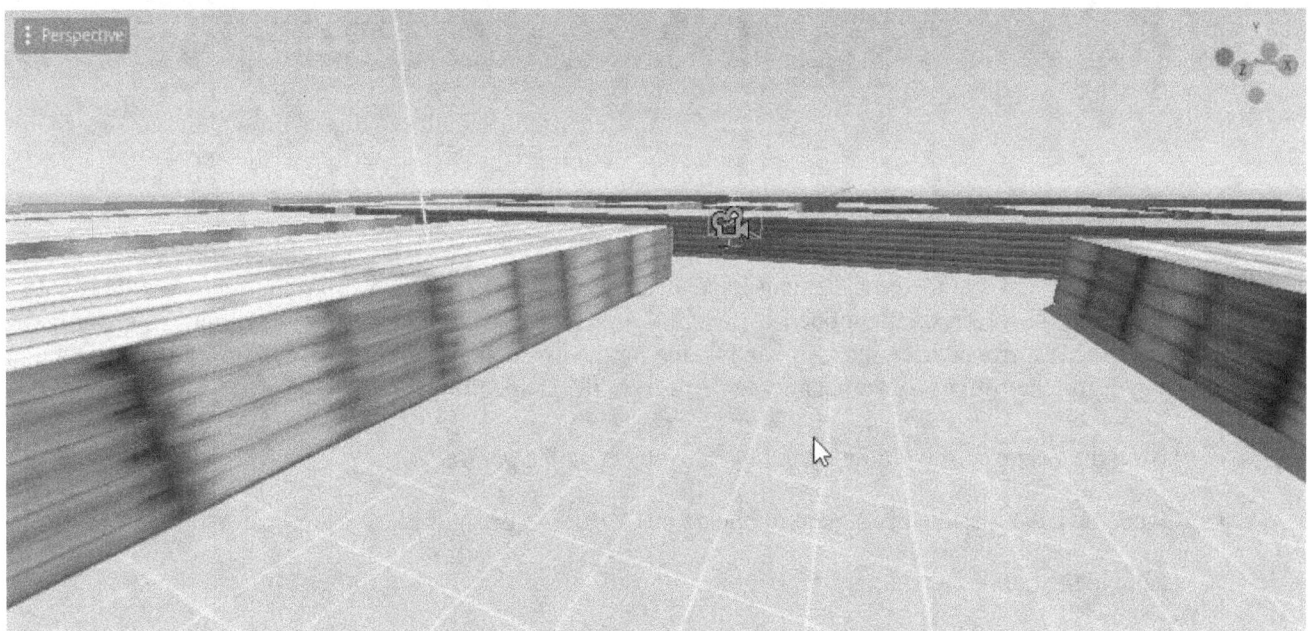

After this change, it is now time to play our scene and navigate around it:

- Press the **Play** button (or **F5***)* (this is to play the scene; you can also press the corresponding button in the top-right corner - the fourth from the left).

- Navigate through the scene, using the arrow keys and the mouse.

- It should look as described on the next figure.

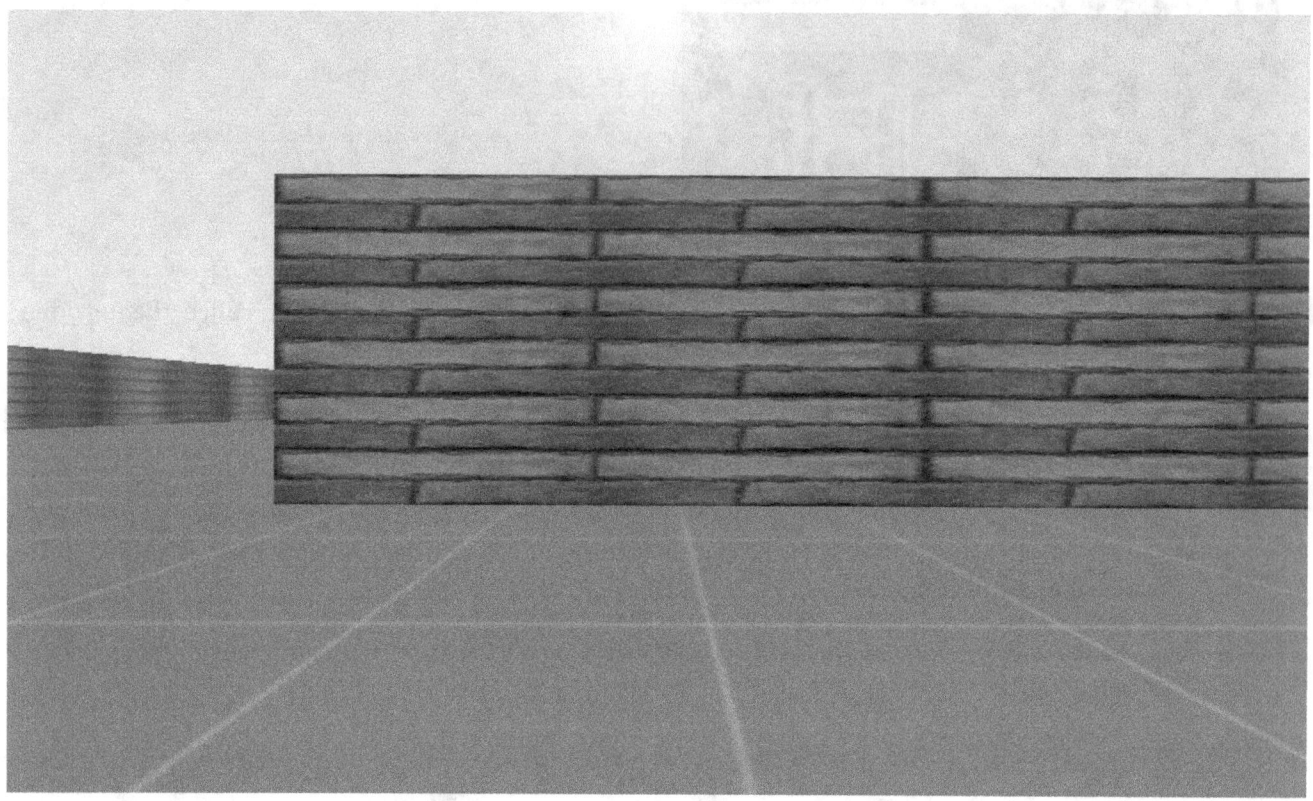

ADDING A CEILING TO THE MAZE

Once you have checked that the environment looks as expected, we can stop playing the scene. At this stage, the level is functional; however, as mentioned earlier, it would be great to also include a ceiling. This can be done easily by copying the ground, moving it up, and changing the associated texture. We will use the same techniques as before (by using the **Move** tool and changing textures in the **Inspector**):

- Using the **SceneTree** window, search for the object called ***ground***.

- Once you have located this object, duplicate it (*CTRL + D* or right-click + duplicate).

- Rename the duplicate **ceiling**.

- Using the **Inspector**, change its position to **(0, 5, 0)**.

Once this is done, we just need to apply a texture to this ceiling:

- If you have not already done so, import the texture called **ceiling** from the folder downloaded from the companion website and save it in a folder of your choice within Godot (e.g., m**aze** | **textures**).

- Select the object called **ceiling**.

- In the Inspector, you will see that its default material is tile (because this object is a duplicate of the ground); so we will need to create and apply a new Material to the ceiling.

- Click on the revolving arrow to the right of the label "Material", this will clear the current texture.

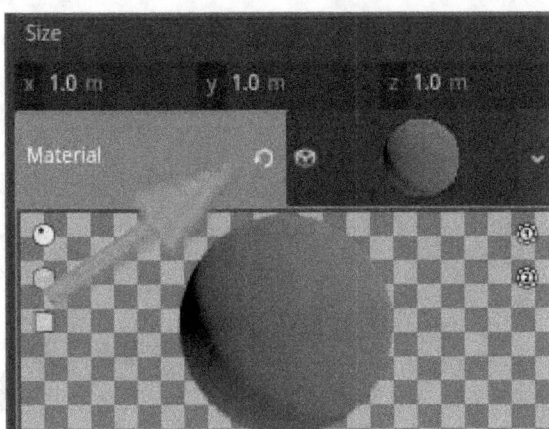

- Then create a new material by clicking on the arrow to the right of the <empty> section, and select the option "**StandardMaterial3D**"

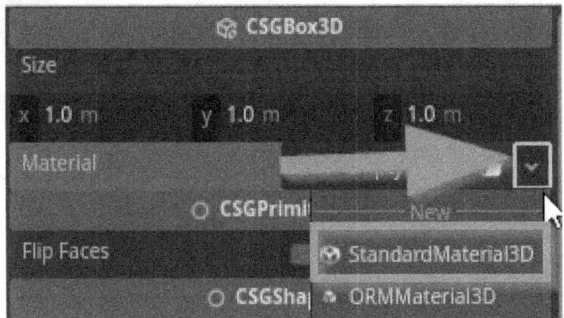

- Using the Albedo field, change the texture of that object using the texture called ceiling.

- You should see that the texture of the ceiling node has now changed.

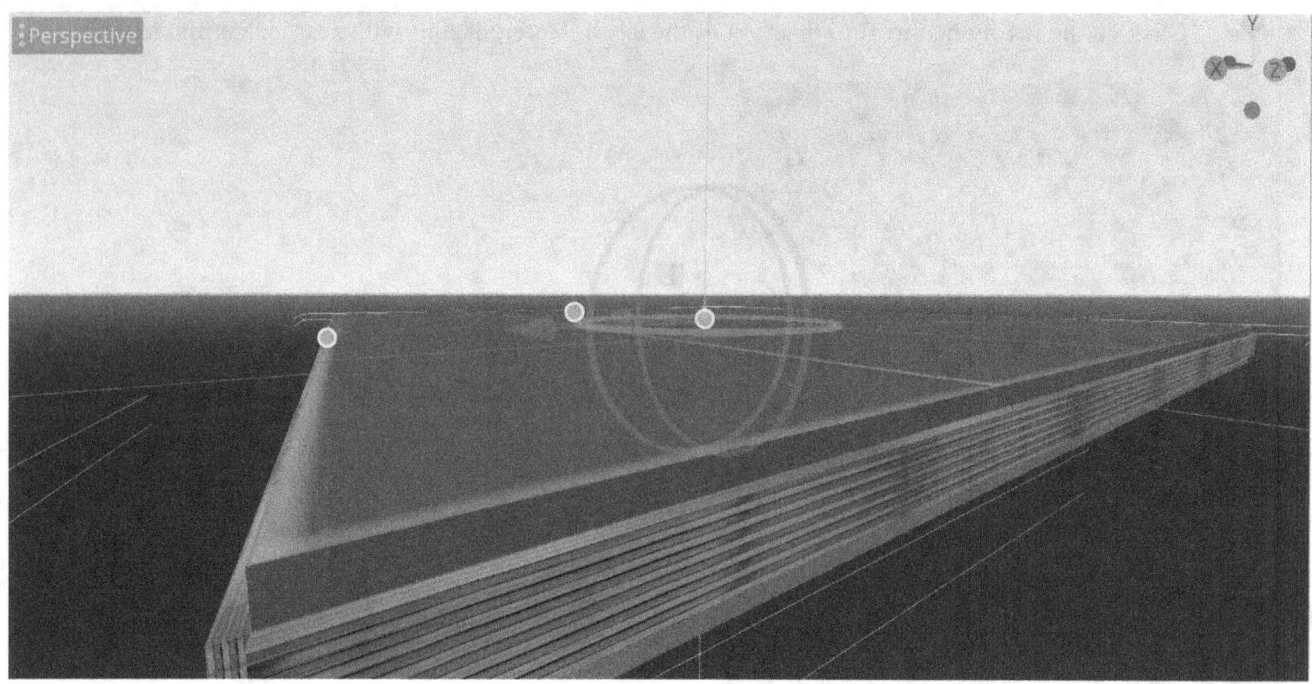

Finally, we will change the tiling properties of this new material by expanding the attribute called **UV1**, and setting its scaling property to **(20, 20, 20)**.

When looking back at the **Scene** view, you can now see that the tiling of the texture for the ceiling has changed, as illustrated in the next screenshot.

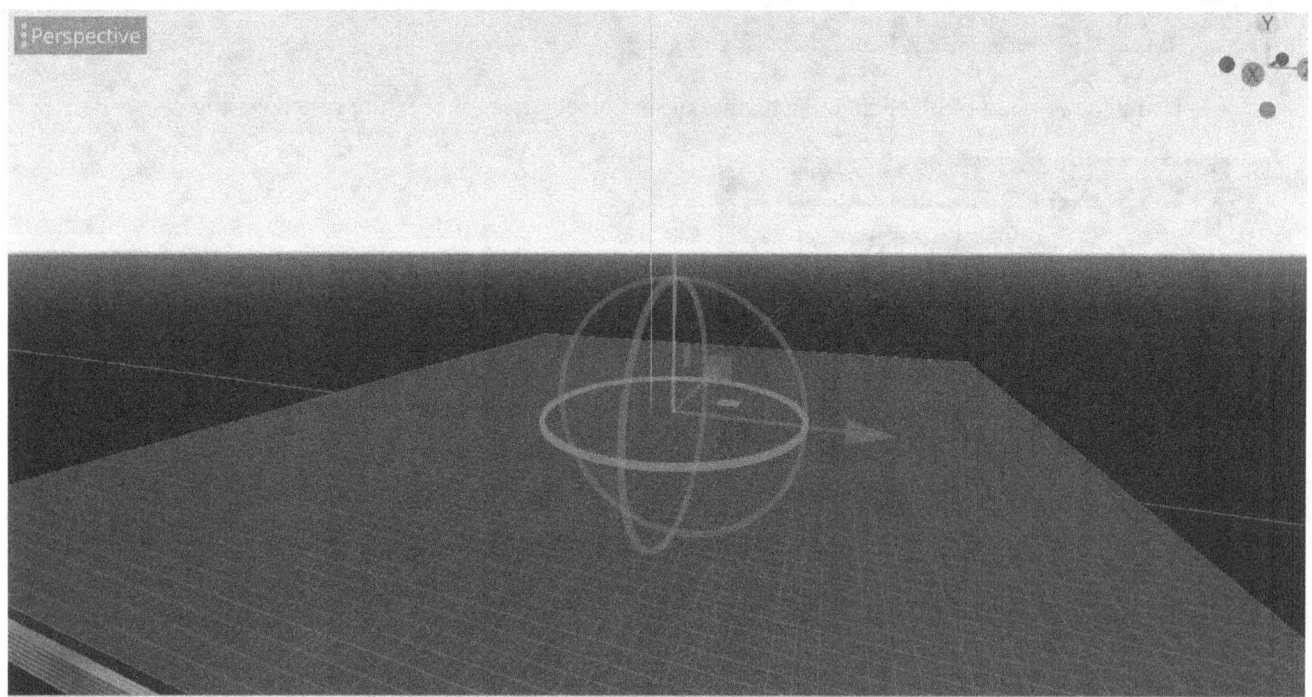

We can now play our scene to see how this new texture looks like, and you may notice that the ceiling looks extremely dark, and this will be solved in the next sections by adding nodes related to light and the environment.

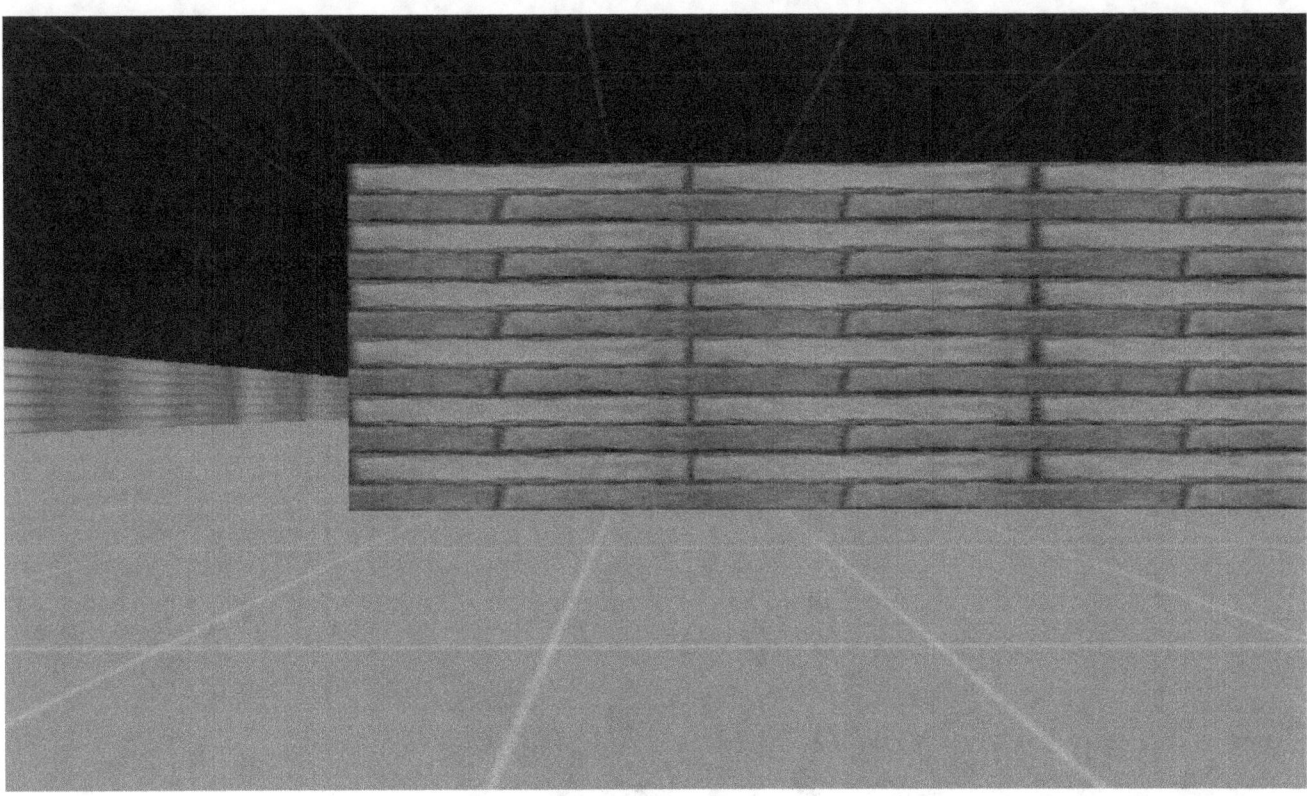

As you navigate through the maze, we may well discover areas that are bright, where the light from outside the maze shines through, indicating that the ceiling is probably not covering the maze entirely. But you can always readjust the size and position of the ceiling at a later stage to ensure that this is fixed.

You may be wondering why you can still see the walls if the environment is perfectly closed. We will see this in more detail later on, but in a nutshell: your scene has default attributes, and some of these are related to the amount of ambient light in the scene. By default, even if no lights have been added to the scene, there will be some ambient light. This, of course, can be modified, and we will do so in the next section.

ADDING LIGHT TO THE SCENE

Once you have amended the maze, we will start adding light to it, to create some dark and bright areas. In your game, this could be used to conceal areas or to highlight rooms or corridors where the player should go.

Before we can add any lights, we will also need to set the properties of the scene's environment, in terms of default lighting and this can be done using the node called **WorldEnvironment**.

- Select the node called Node3D in the **Scene Tree**.

- Add a child of type **WorldEnvironment** to this node, as we have done previously (i.e., select the node, right-click and select **Add Child Node**).

- This will create a node called **WorldEnvironment**.

- Select this node, and, using the **Inspector** window, locate the section called **WorldEnvironment**.

- Click on the arrow to the right of the label called **Environment**, and select the option **Environment** from the contextual menu, as illustrated in the next figure.

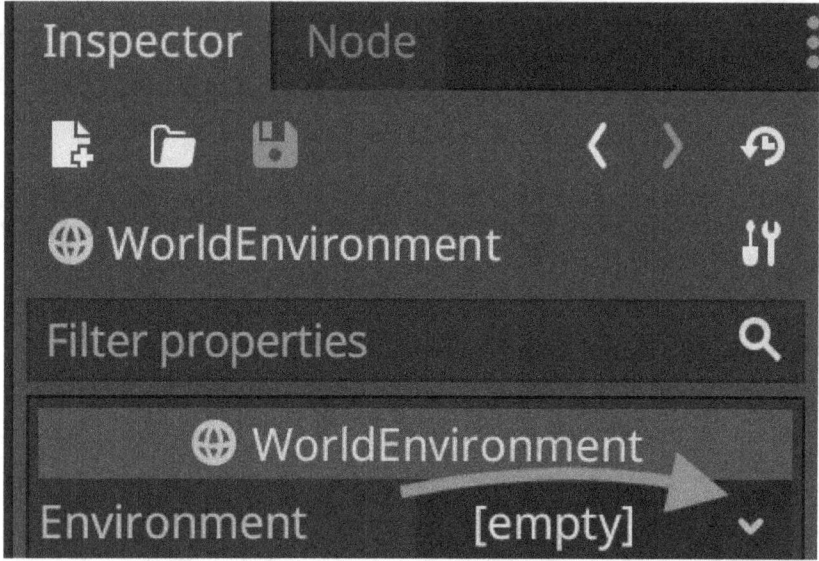

- Click on the item called Environment, as per the next figure. This will show properties linked to the environment.

- Modify the attribute **Background | Mode** to **Custom Color**; by default, a black color will be applied.

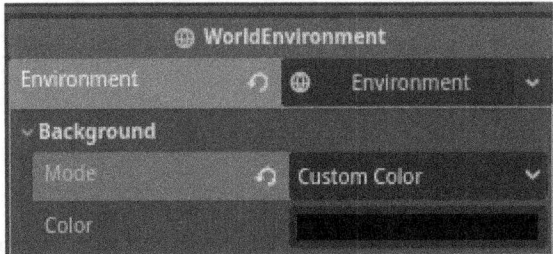

You should now see that the scene is completely dark, and this is normal.

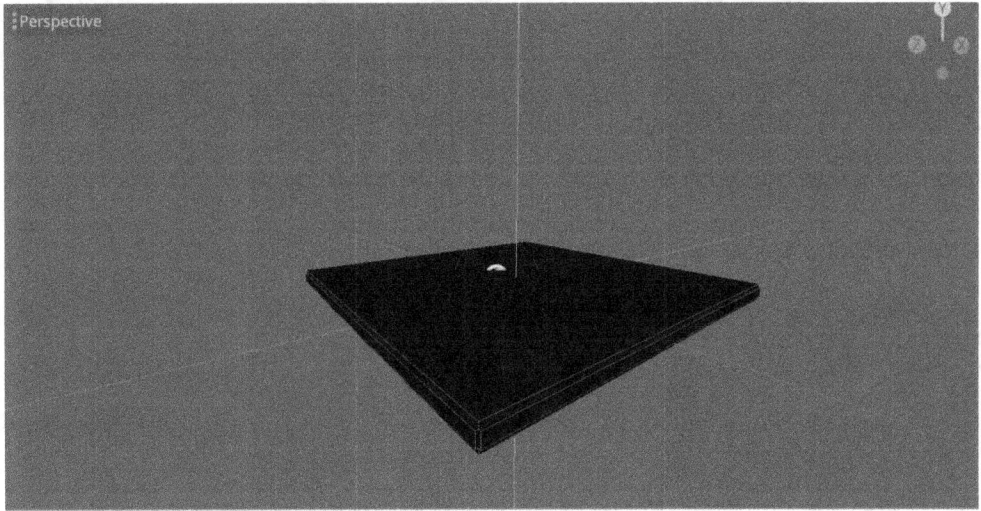

Now that we have added a **WorldEnvironment** node, we can modify its properties to add ambient light.

Next, we will add some lights. There are many different types of lights in Godot, and for the time being, we will just use **Point Lights** to simulate the light created from a bulb, or a torch light, that shines from a specific point in all directions.

Because the ceiling is now the top-most object when looking at the scene from the y-axis, we can temporarily deactivate it so that it is easier to add and move objects within the maze. To do so:

- In the **Scene** dock, select the object labeled **ceiling** in the **Scene Tree**.

- Toggle its visibility to invisible using the eye icon that appears to the right of the node.

Once this is done, we can start to add lights to the scene:

- Select the node called **Node3D**.

- Right-click on this node and add a new node of type **OmniLight3D.**

- Change its **y** coordinate to **2**.

- You can move this light near the player so that you can see the impact it has on the scene immediately.

- In the **Inspector**, locate the section called **Omni**, and change the range to **20**.

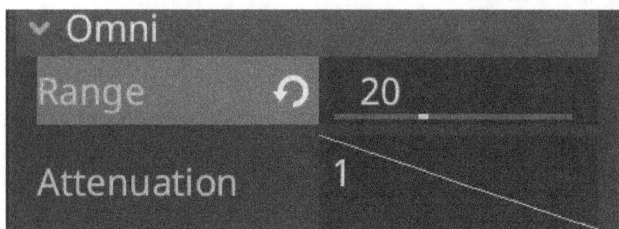

- Similarly, locate the section called **Light**, and change the energy to **5**.

- You should now see a new object labeled **OmniLight3D** in the **SceneTree** as well as a new light in the **ViewPort**.

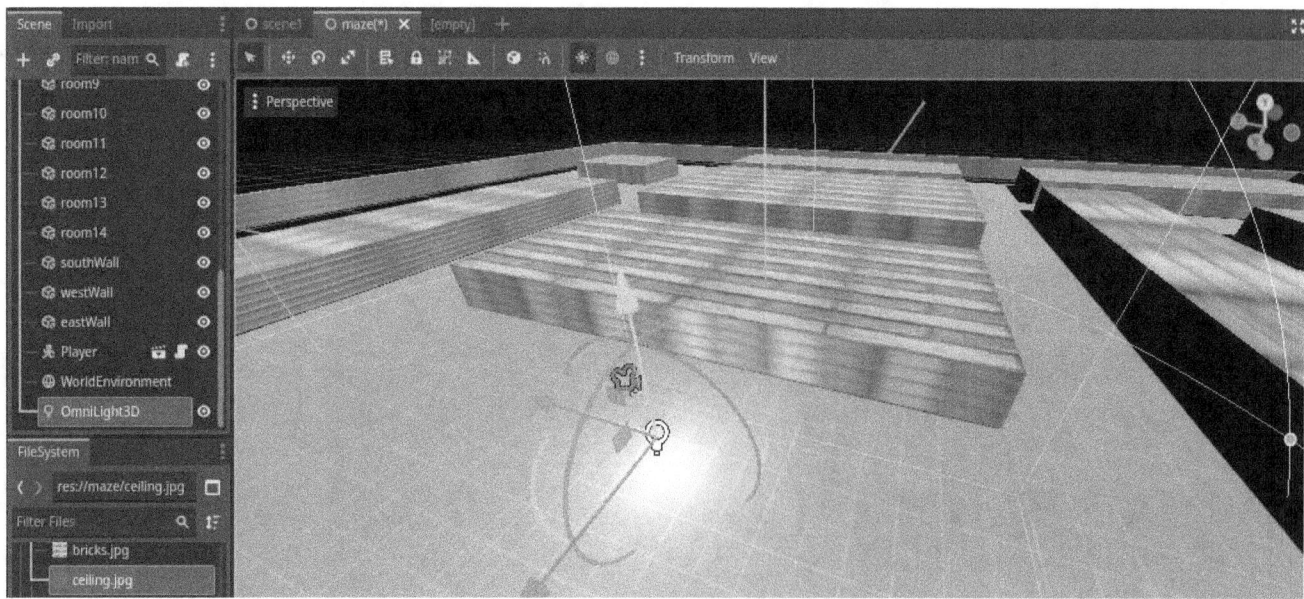

- You can also reactivate the ceiling.

- You can play the scene that should now look like the following figure.

Navigating the scene without external light

After checking the scene, we can reproduce the last steps to include more lights, by either duplicating and moving the **OmniLight3D** that we have created, or by adding more **OmniLight3D** nodes as children of the node **Node3D** as follows:

- Temporarily deactivate the **ceiling**: this will make it easier to move the lights.

- Duplicate the node **OmniLight3D** that you have created previously several times to locations of your choice, making sure that most corridors are lit up properly.

- Move the duplicates to different locations in the maze.

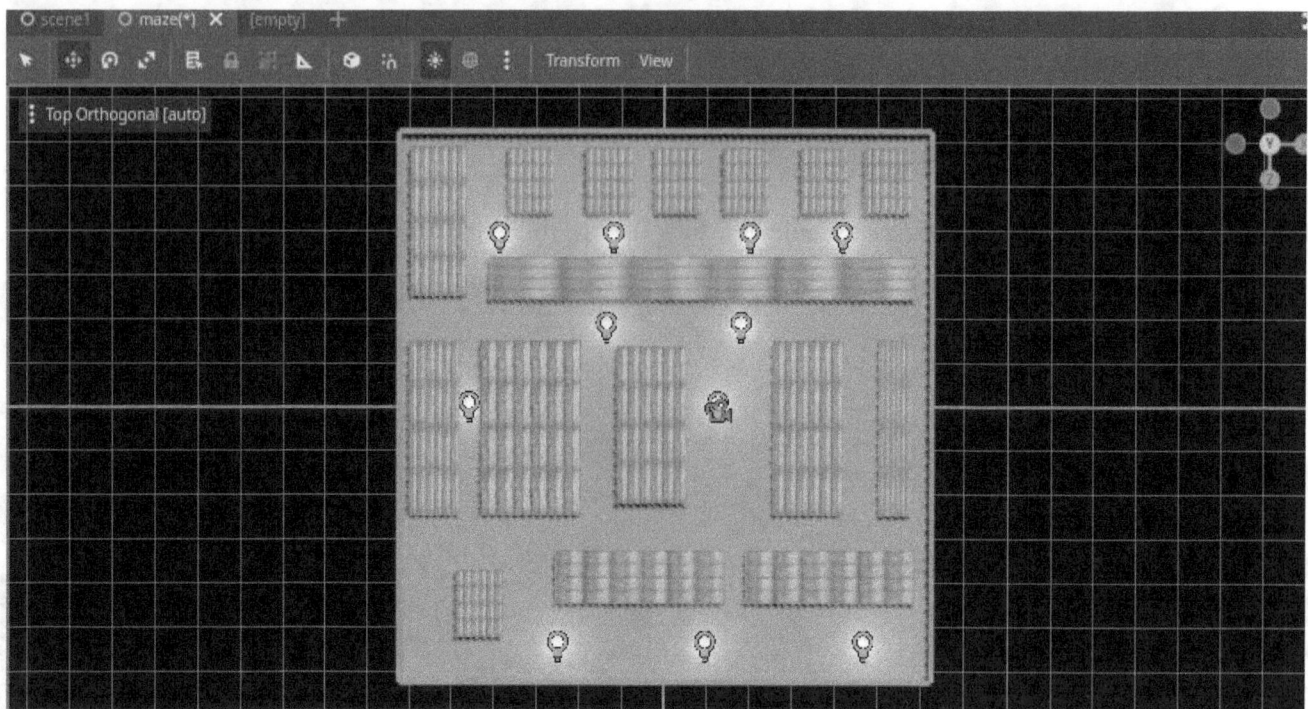

- Modify the settings for each light and amend their **Range**, **Energy,** or **Color** to create special effects of your choice (e.g., each with a different color and intensity).

- Reactivate the ceiling, play the scene and see how it looks like.

As you can see on the next picture, the lights can be used to highlight points of interest.

LEVEL ROUNDUP

Summary

In this chapter, we have become more comfortable with the creation of an indoor environment and we learned how to create a maze from built-in objects such as boxes, point lights, or cameras. We also used the skills acquired in the previous sections to transform objects and to create a fully functional level.

Quiz

It is now time to test your knowledge. The solutions are on the next page.

1. The shortcut to move an object is Q.

2. The shortcut to rotate an object is R.

3. The **Ambient Lighting** can be modified using the menu **Project Settings**.

4. **Energy** is an attribute of **OmniLights**.

5. If no lights have been added to the scene, the scene will be completely dark.

6. New objects are always created at the position **(0, 0, 0)**.

7. **UV1** is one of the attributes of texture materials used in a scene.

8. Once a texture has been applied to an object it cannot be replaced later.

9. A scaling property of **(1, 1, 1)** means that the picture will be repeated once on all the x-, y and z-axes.

10. The shortcut *CTRL +D* is used to delete an object.

Solutions to the Quiz

1. FALSE.

2. FALSE

3. TRUE.

4. TRUE.

5. FALSE (ambient light can be used instead).

6. TRUE.

7. TRUE.

8. FALSE.

9. TRUE.

10. FALSE.

Checklist

You can move to the next chapter if you can do the following:

- Apply a template to create a scene.

- Duplicate objects.

- Move and transform objects to create a maze.

- Change the tiling property of a texture.

- Add lights to a scene.

- Modify the intensity/energy and the color of the default ambient light for a scene.

Challenge 1

For this challenge, you will need to create a new maze based on a new template as follows:

- Import the texture **gameMap2.png** from the folder that you have downloaded from the companion site.

- Apply the techniques covered in this chapter to recreate the maze based on this outline.

- Add lights at locations of your choice.

Challenge 2

For this challenge, you will need to create your own outline using the image manipulation tool of your choice and then apply it to create a totally new maze of your own design!

You could proceed as follows:

- Create a new image with a size of 100 pixels by 100 pixels.

- Set the background colour to white and the foreground colour to black.

- Create the maze using a brush of size **1**.

- Save your image in the **png** or **jpg** format.

- Import this image into Godot.

- Create a new scene and use this new template to create your own new maze.

CHAPTER 5: CREATING AN OUTDOOR SCENE WITH GODOT'S BUILT-IN TERRAIN GENERATOR

In this chapter, we will start to use Godot's built-in packages to create an outdoor scene and to navigate through it using different types of vehicles.

After completing this section, you should be able to:

- Create a realistic landscape from a template.

- Create a terrain and modify it to produce hills and valleys.

THE PLAN

For this chapter, we will create an island through which you will be able to navigate. So the plan is quite straight-forward, and we will do the following:

- Import a template that we will use to draw the outline of the environment.

- Create a terrain based on this template.

- Paint over the template.

- Create hills and valleys.

- Add trees and other types of foliage.

- Add buildings based on boxes.

The next screenshot is a preview of what you will have accomplished after completing this chapter.

THE ISLAND OUTLINE

For this level, we will be creating an island. As per the previous chapter, we will be using an image created in Photoshop to define its outline and the main features.

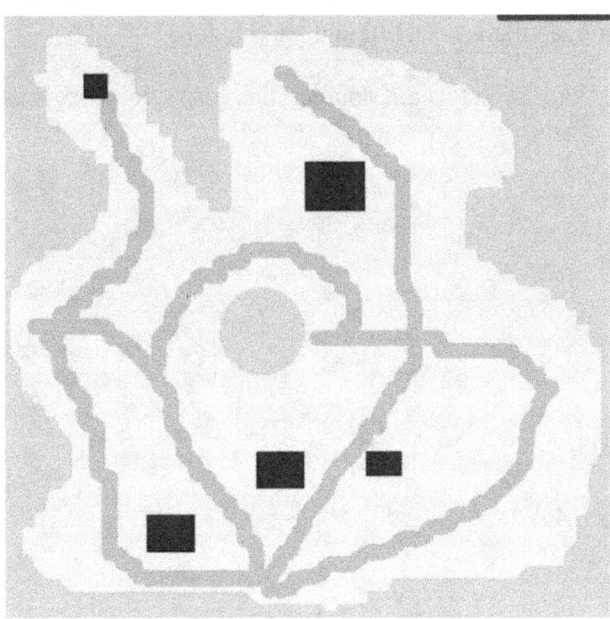

The outline of the island

As you can see, this is a rather coarse outline, but it gives an idea of the shape of the island. You may notice the following:

- Water surrounding the island in blue.

- Sand for most of the island.

- Brown patches to highlight paths.

- Green dots to identify the location of the trees.

- Black rectangles to indicate the position of buildings.

- A lake symbolized by a blue circle in the middle of the island.

This image is 500 pixels by 500 pixels and it will be mapped so that 1 pixel roughly equates to 1 meter in Godot. If you want to create your own outline, you can do so easily using these settings. The map does not have to be extremely detailed because, as you will see later, we will be able to paint over it and to also remove (or erase) some of its elements. What is important for now is that you have an outline that you can use directly in Godot.

IMPORTING NECESSARY ASSETS

At this stage, we are ready to start with our island. If you remember well, we will be adding trees and a terrain that will mimic the shape of the island. For this purpose, we need to import specific packages to be able to complete these tasks. These packages include a terrain asset.

- In Godot, create a new scene (**Scene | New Scene**).

- Open the **AssetLib** window by clicking on the button labelled **AssetLib** in the top menu.

- In the search field, type "**Heightmap terrain**" and select (i.e., double-click on) the asset called **Heightmap terrain**.

- In the next window, click on the button labelled **Download**.

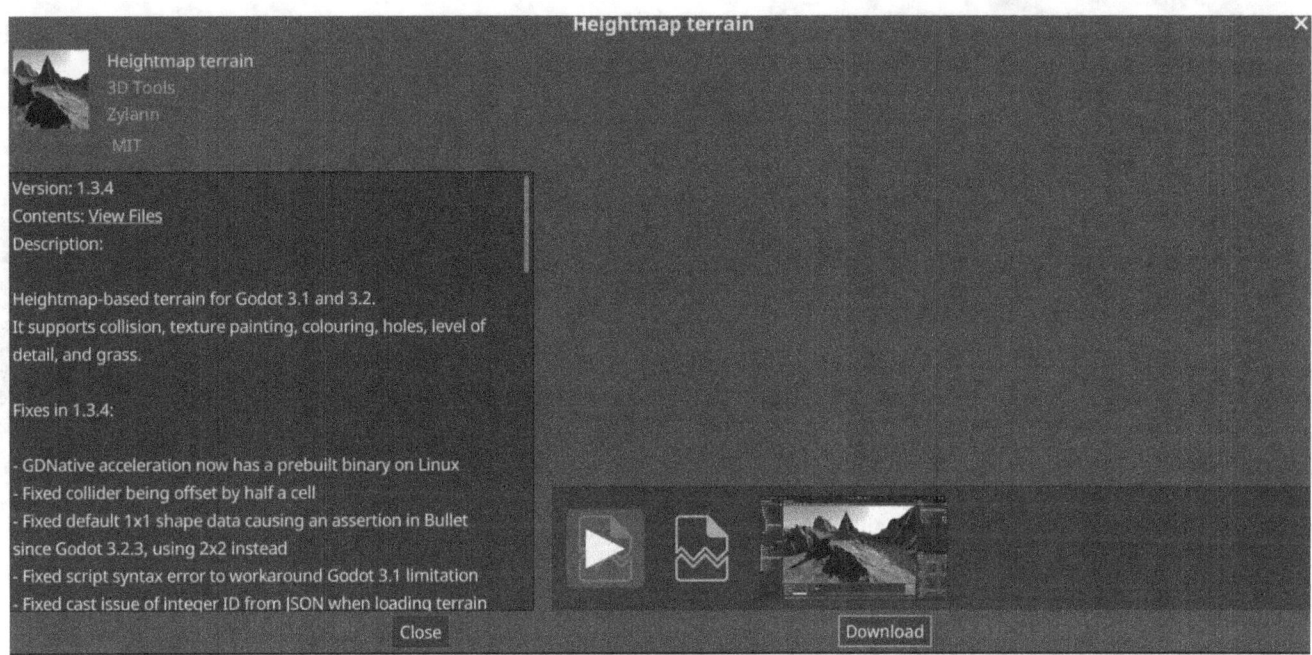

- Once the library has been downloaded click on the button labelled "**Install ...**".

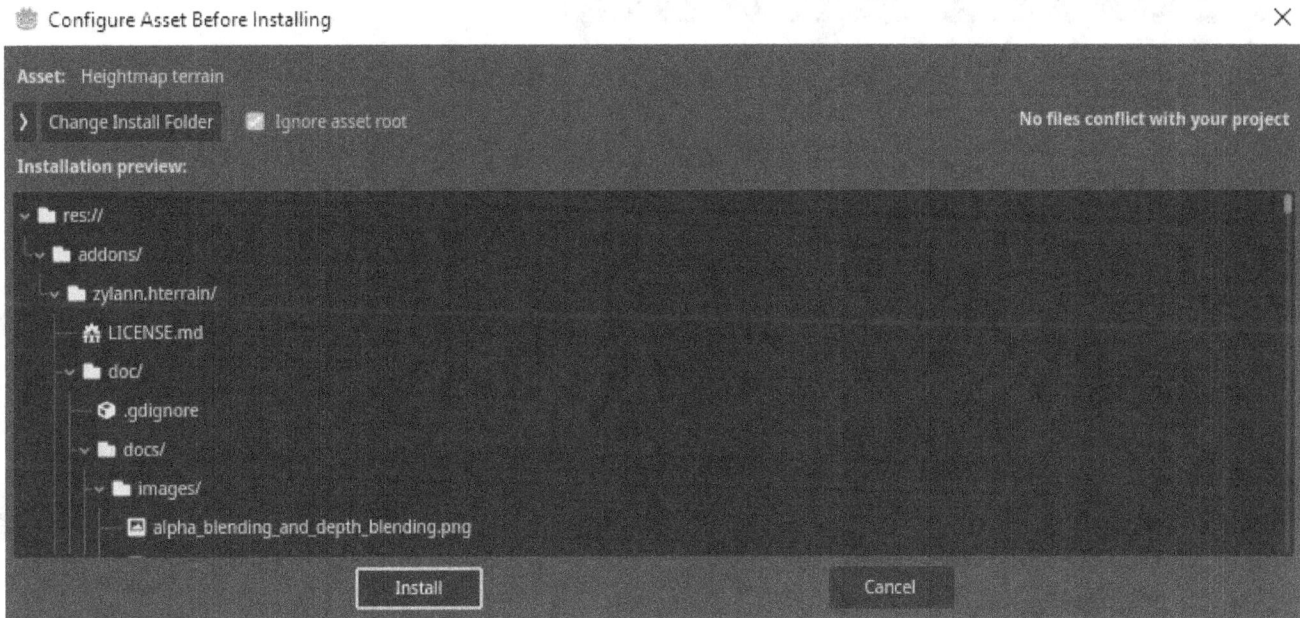

- Once the installation is complete, you should see a folder called **addons | zylann.hterrain** in the **FileSystem** window.

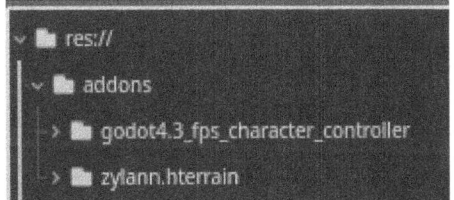

We now need to activate this plugin; to do so, select **Project | Project Settings | Plugins** and set the status of this plugin to **Enabled**, by clicking on the **On** option, as illustrated in the next figure.

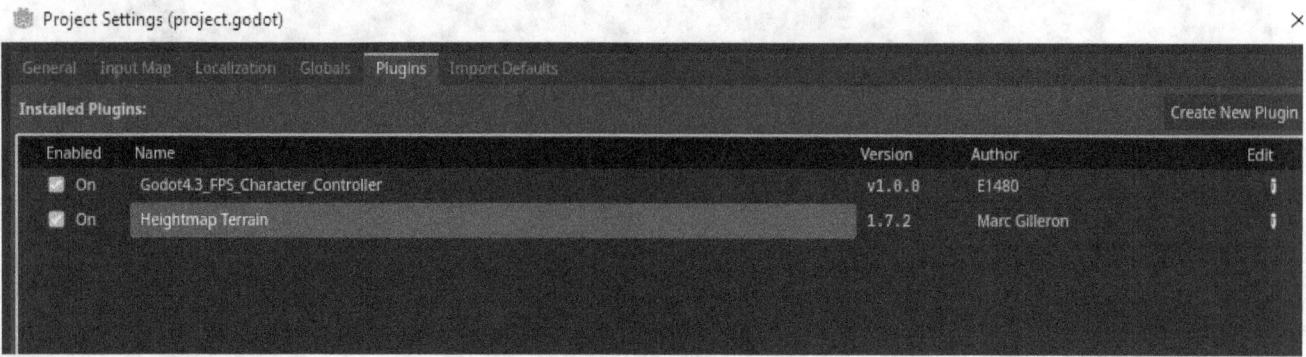

Now that the plugin is active, we can start to create our terrain.

- Select the 3D view/workspace by clicking on the button labelled "**3D**" in the top menu.

- In the **Scene** dock, click on **3D Scene**, this will create a new node called **Node3D**.

- Press **CTRL + A** (to add new node), type **terrain** in the search field and select the node type **HTerrain** from the list.

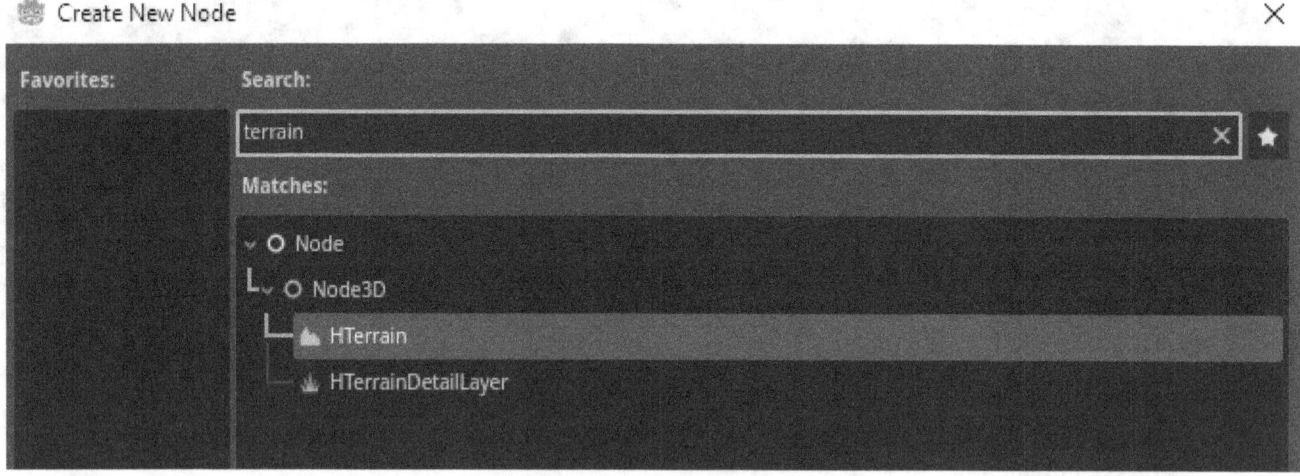

- This will create a new object called **HTerrain** in the **Scene Tree**.

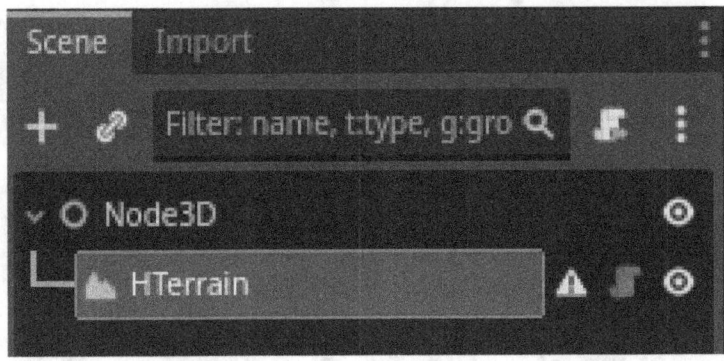

As you will see, a warning sign will appear to the right of the node **HTerrain**. So that we can store the data generated by the terrain, we need to create a folder and to associate it with the new terrain, so do the following:

- Using the **FileSystem** dock, create a new folder: right-click on **res://**, select the option **New Folder** from the contextual menu, and give this new folder a name, for example **terrainData**.

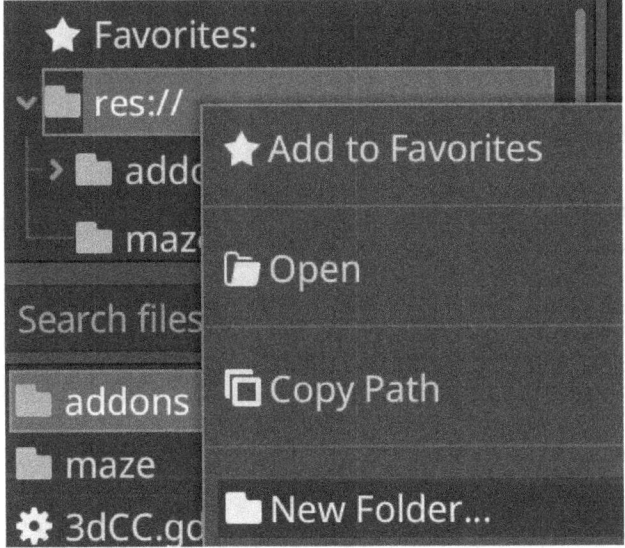

- Select the node **HTerrain** in the **Scene Tree**.

- Using the **Inspector**, locate the attribute called **Data Directory** in the section **HTerrain**.

- Click on the folder logo to the right of the attribute **Data Directory**.

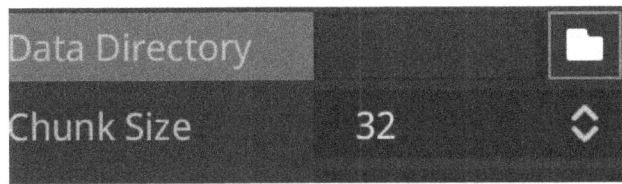

- Choose the folder that you have just created (e.g., **terrainData**); this folder is necessary to save the terrain's data.

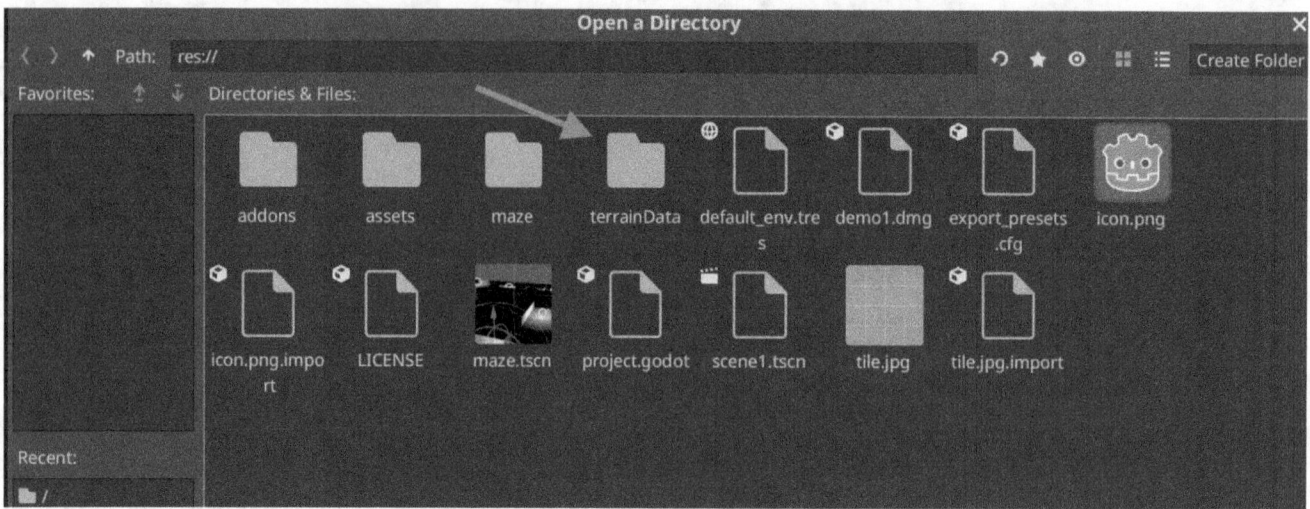

- Click on the button labelled "**Select Folder**"

Once this is done, we can start to create hills and valleys for this terrain.

If you select the **HTerrain** object in the **Scene Tree**, you will notice a window at the bottom of the screen that includes tools that can be used to modify the terrain, as illustrated in the next figure.

Amongst other things, this window will make it possible to apply textures to the terrain and to lower or raise areas within.

So, at this stage we have all the necessary assets to create our island, except from the outline map. So let's import it:

- Switch to your file system (e.g., explorer or Finder).

- Locate the folder where you have downloaded the resource pack at the start of this book.

- Select the file labeled **gameMapOutline.png**.

- Drag and drop this file inside the **FileSystem** dock in Godot.

CREATING THE OUTLINE OF THE ISLAND

At this stage, we have most of the assets that we require to start. So let's create the terrain:

- Select the node called **HTerrain** in the **Scene Tree**.

- Click on the button called **Edit** located at the bottom of the window.

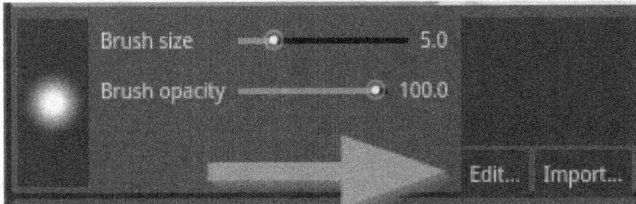

In the new window, click on the + button located on the left-hand side of the scree to create a new texture.

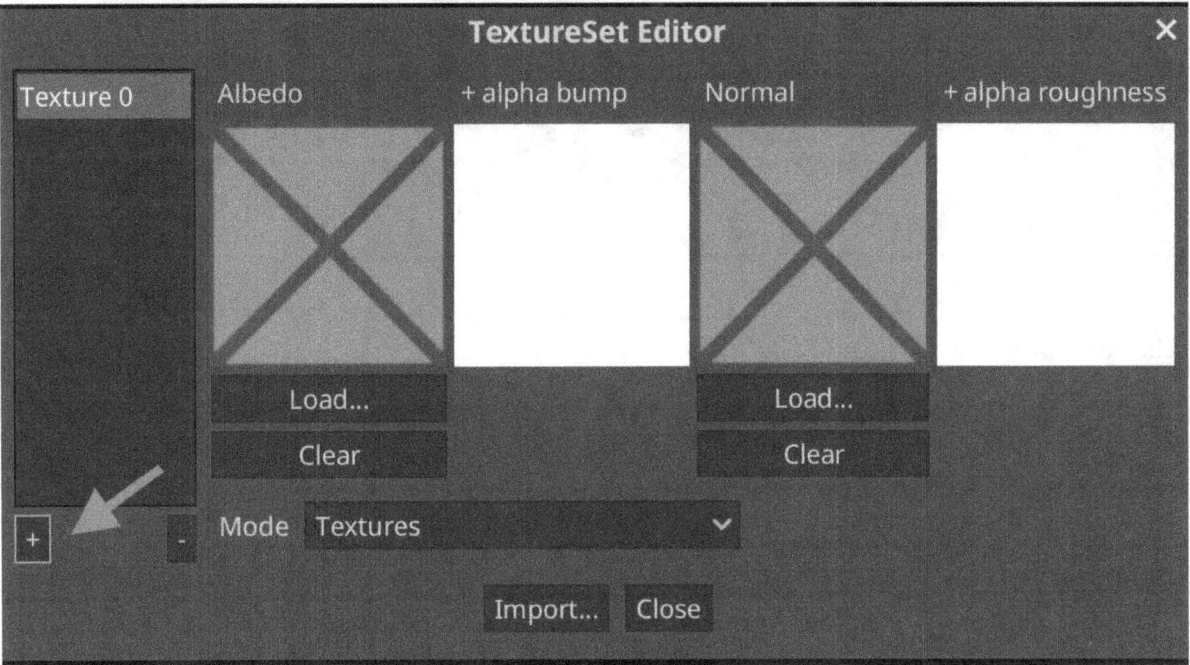

- This will create a texture called **Texture 0**.

- Next, click on the button labelled "**Load**", just below the section called **Albedo**.

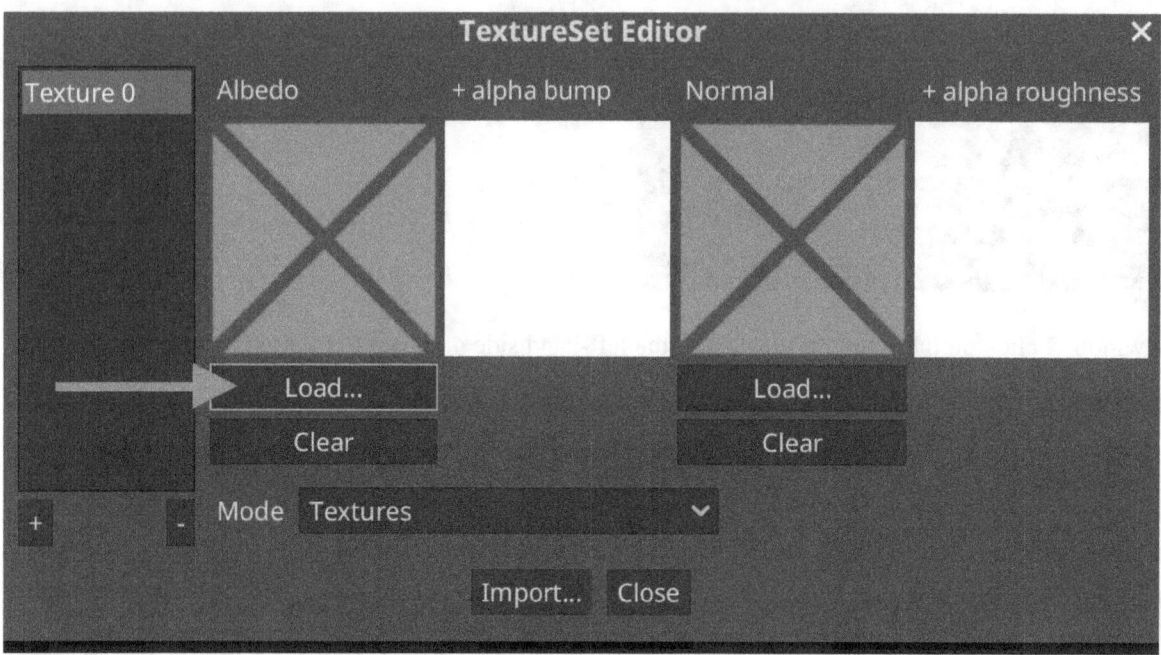

- In the new window, select the texture that we have imported previously called **gameOutline.png** and then click on **Open**.

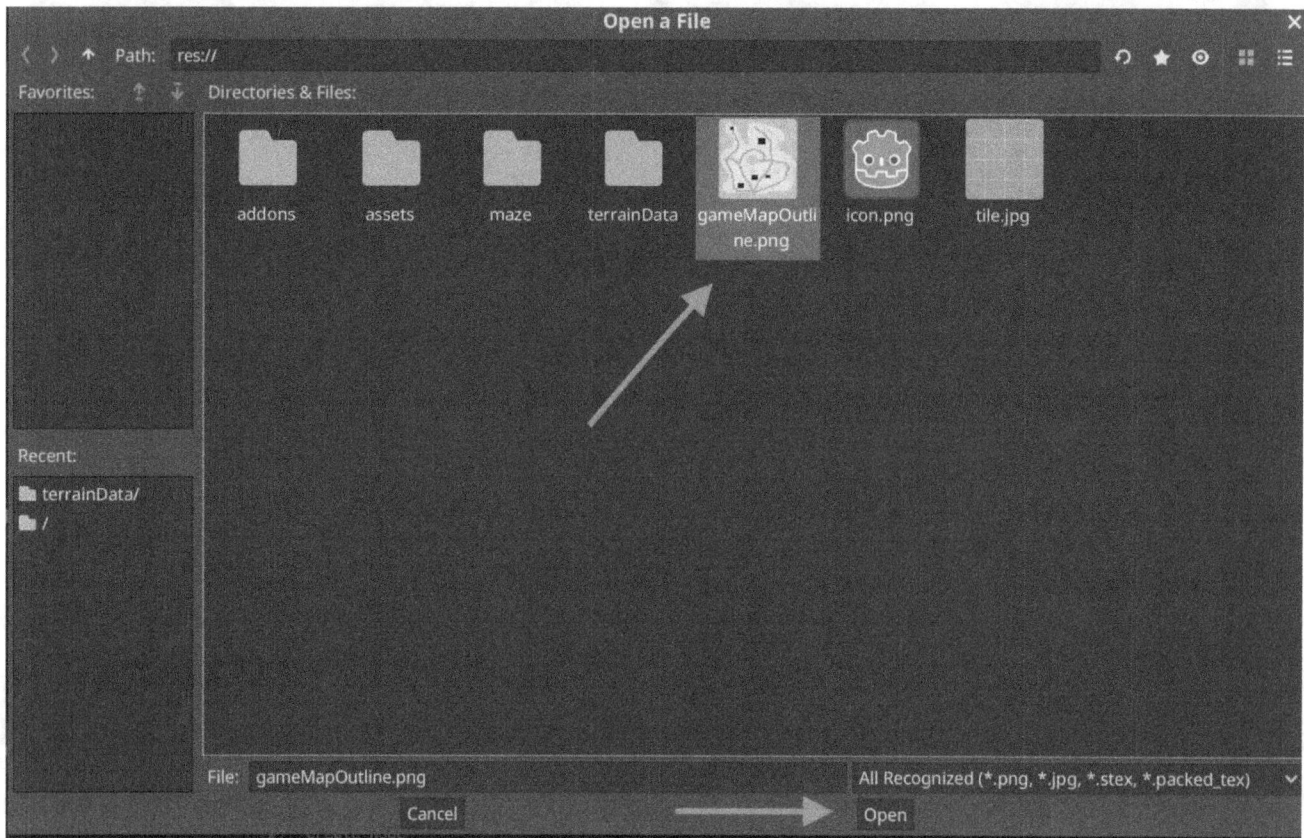

- You should see in the next window that this texture has been selected and you can now press the button labelled **Close**.

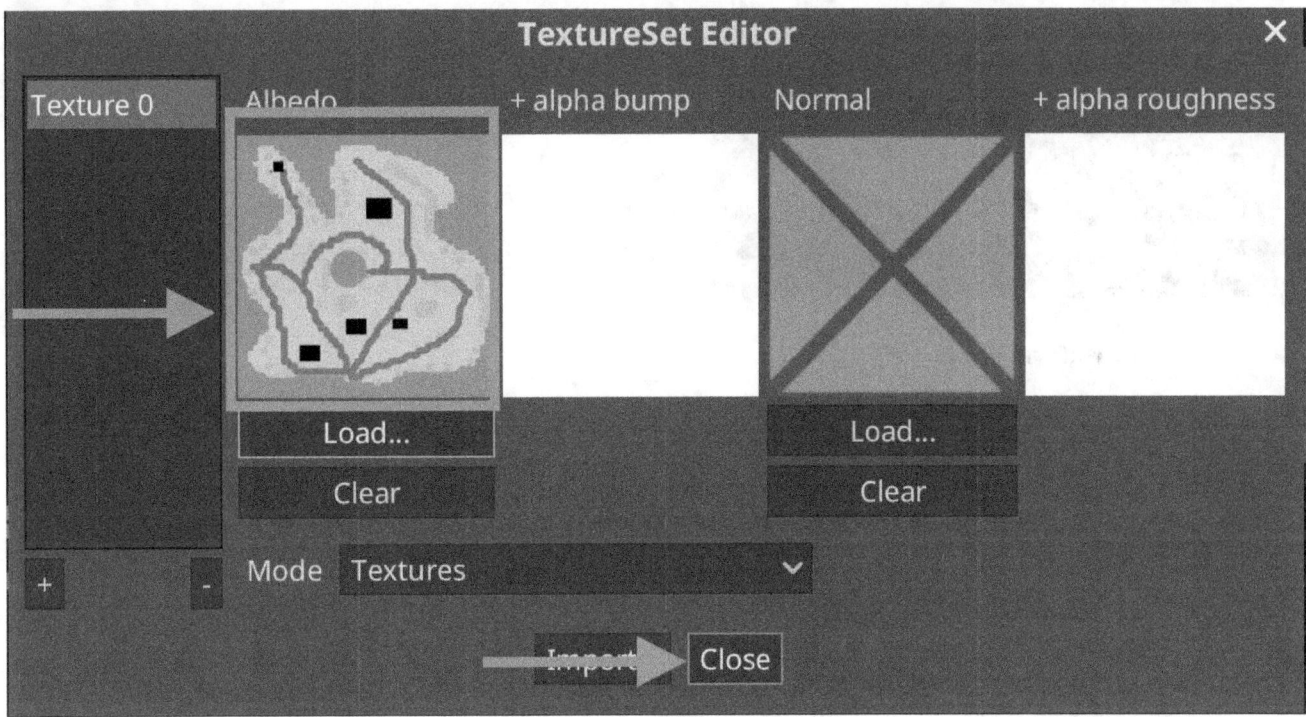

If you now look at the **ViewPort**, you should see that his texture is repeated several times over the terrain.

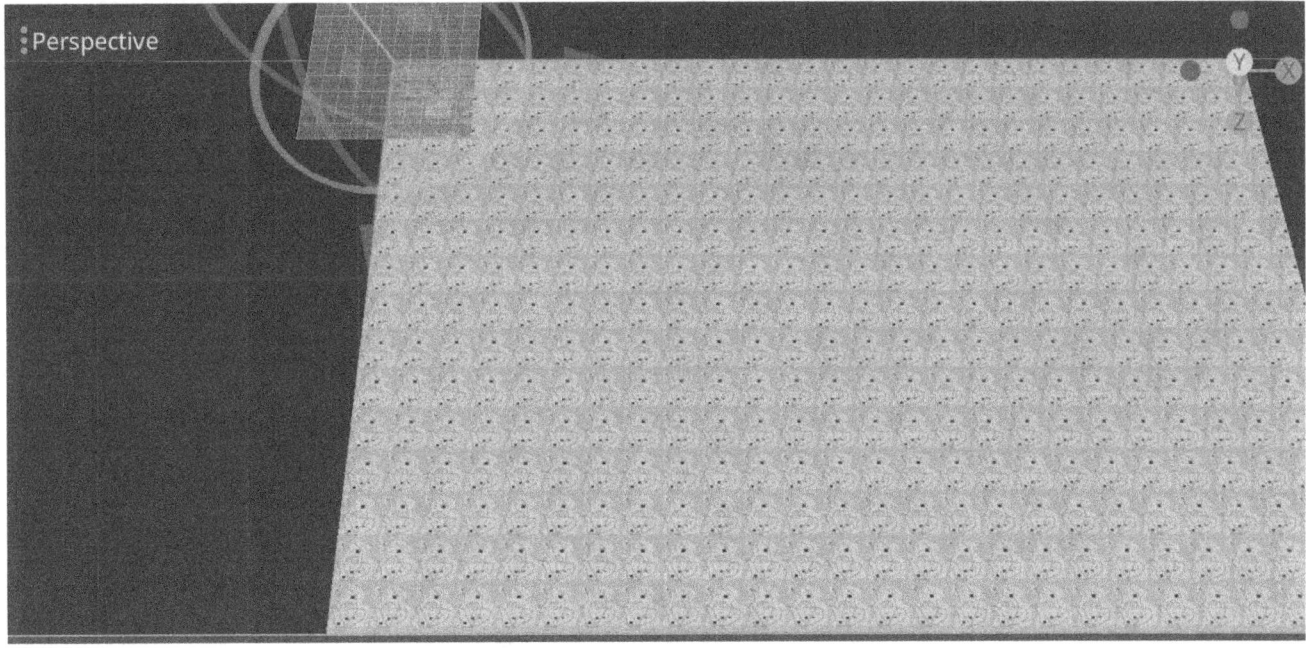

However, we want it to be displayed only once; so we will need to modify the tiling of this texture:

- Select the object **HTerrain**.

- In the **Inspector**, set the the attributes MapScale to (1,1,1) and Centered to On

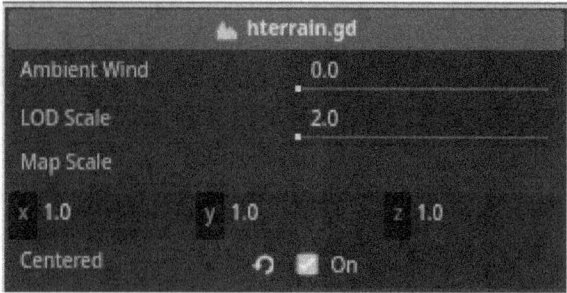

- Set **Trasnform | Scale** to **(1,1,1)**

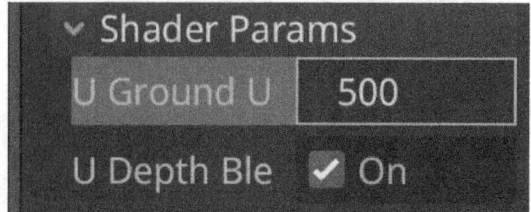

- Once this is done, you should now see that the texture is applied only once to the terrain.

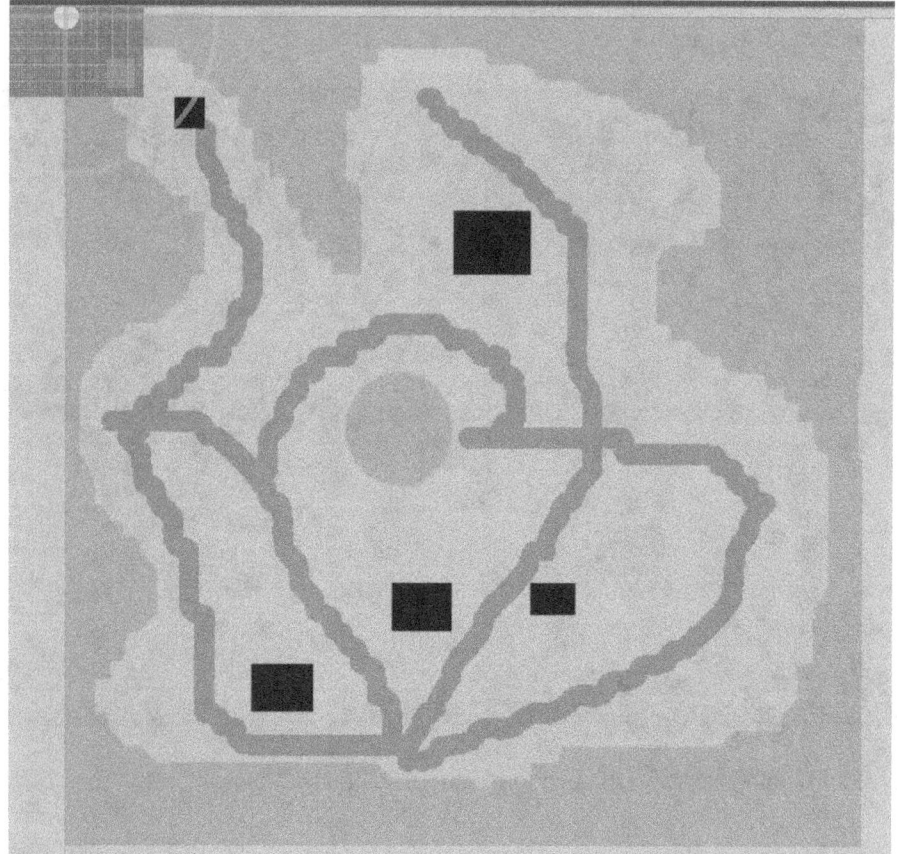

Now that we have the outline we can start to raise or lower parts of the terrain. To do so, we will be using some of the tools available in the top-right corner of the viewport.

GIVING DEPTH TO THE TERRAIN

So far, we have managed to apply the outline of the island, and that's great. It is now time to add some depth to the terrain.

do the following:

- Make sure that the node **HTerrain** is selected.

- Using the top tool bar, select the **Lower Height** tool (second from the left).

- Change the opacity of your brush to **100%**.

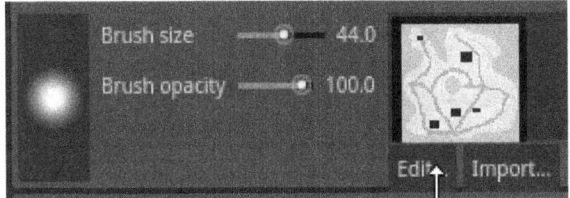

- You can switch to a more convenient view so that we can see the scene from the **y-axis**: locate the **Gizmo** in the **ViewPort** view and click on its **y-axis**. This should switch the view accordingly.

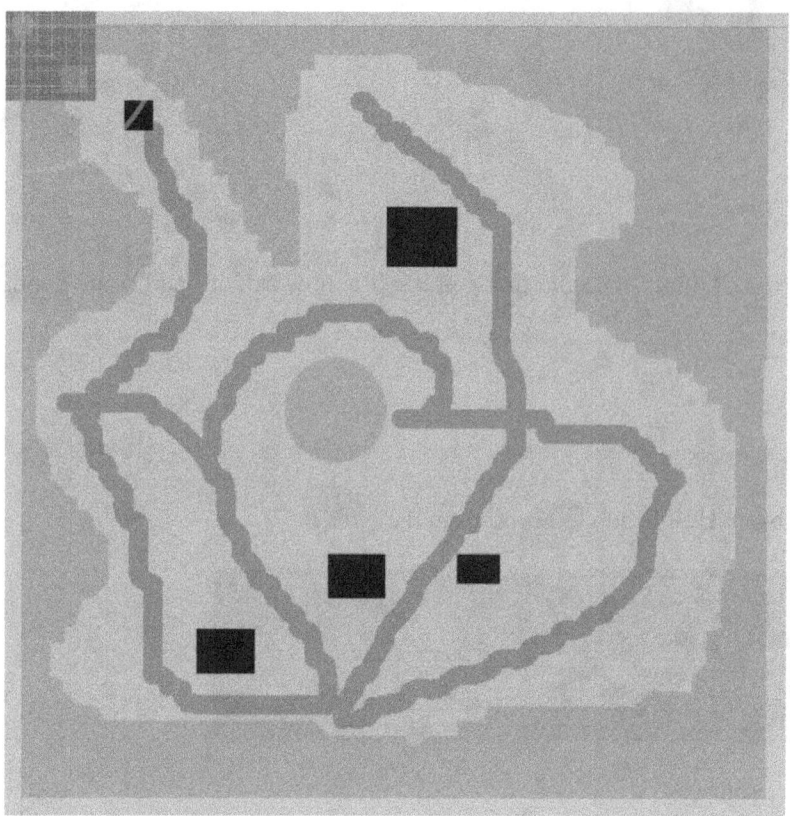

The island viewed from the y-axis

- You might as well zoom-in on the bottom right corner of the terrain using successively the mouse wheel and the **Pan** tool (*SHIFT + drag and drop*).

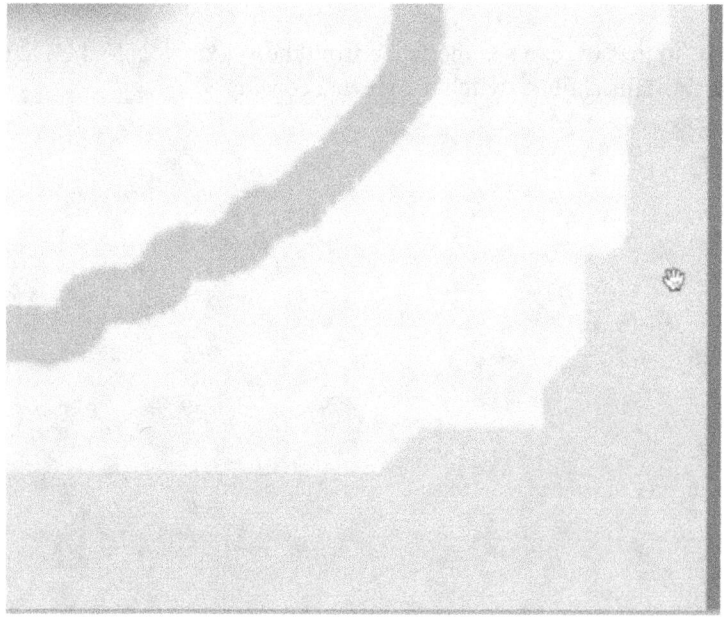

Zooming-in on the southeast coast

- In the **ViewPort**, start to drag and drop your mouse on the blue area and modify the brush size to **11** if necessary (to cover a wider area). As you do so, you will notice chunks of the terrain disappearing, as described in the next figure.

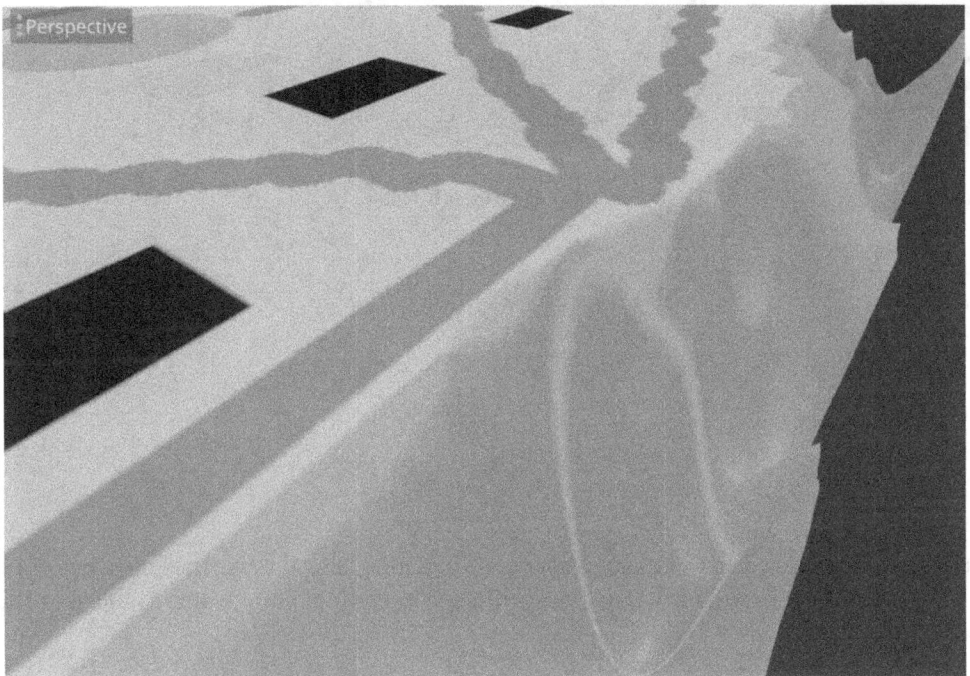

- Carry on until you have covered most of the water area around the island.

Once you have completed the entire outline for the island, we can smooth out the edges to make it look a bit neater and polish-up our work.

- After ensuring that the node **HTerrain** has been selected, select the **Smooth Height** tool (third from the left).

- Select a brush of your choice and set the brush size to **15**.

- After adjusting these settings, you can apply the brush to the edges created from the previous tool, and you will notice that these are nicely smoothed out.

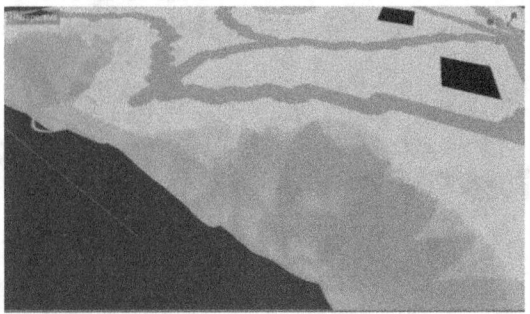

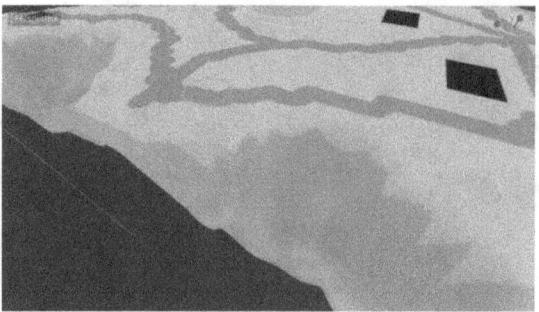

The island before the Smooth tool

The island after the Smooth tool

ADDING WATER

At this stage, the outline has been applied and the boundary between the island and the water is clearly defined. So we can now introduce the **Water** asset. In the next steps, we will successively add the water to the scene and adjust it to ensure that the scene is realistic:

- Create a new **CSGCylinder3D** node as a child of the node **Node3D**, and call that bode **water**.

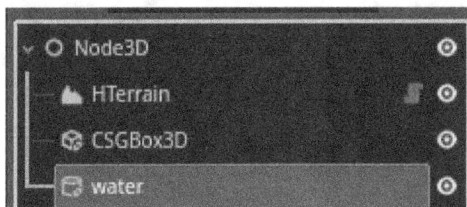

- Using the Inspector, change its number of sides to 15 using the attribute Sides.

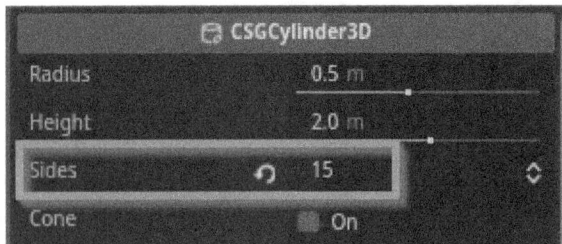

- Change its color to a light blue by creating a new Material, as you have done in the previous sections.

- Change its position to **(0, -10, 0)** and its scale to **(1000,1,1000)**.

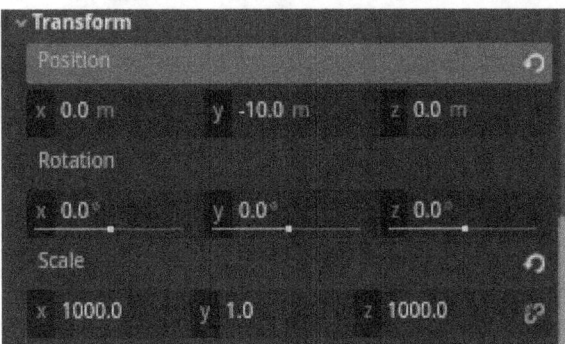

- To add transparency to the water, set the **CSGCylinder3D | Transparency** attribute to **Alpha**.

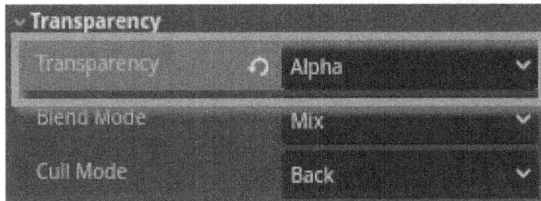

- Set the **Alpha** property of the attribute **Albedo | Color** to **100**.

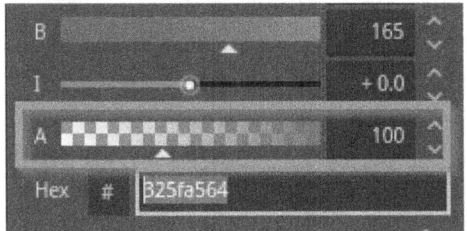

- You should see that the cylinder that represents the water is now transparent.

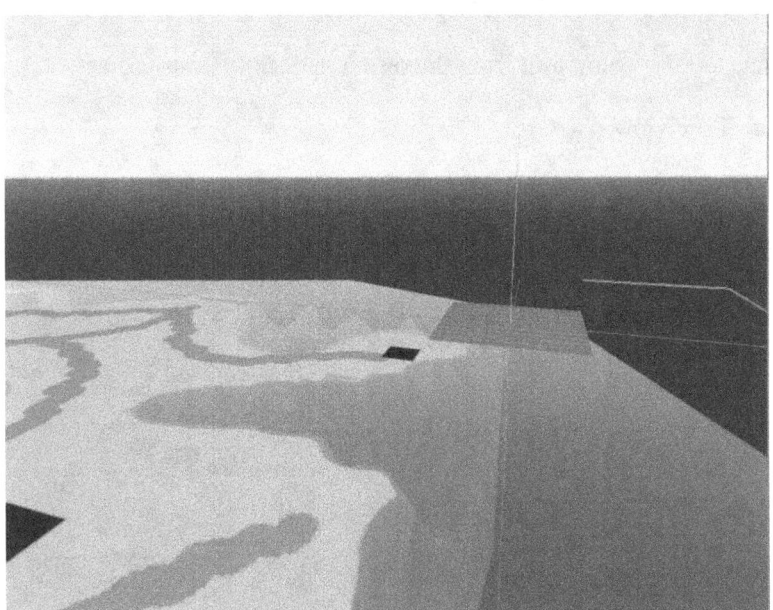

- Using the **Move** tool, move this object up or down so that it appears at the boundary that you have just smoothed-out previously (see the boundary highlighted on the next figure): this will take some readjusting and you don't need to have it right the first time. In fact, if some blue color (from the texture of the ground) still appears above the water, we will be able to erase it later on, and replace it by a texture that is similar to the sand instead.

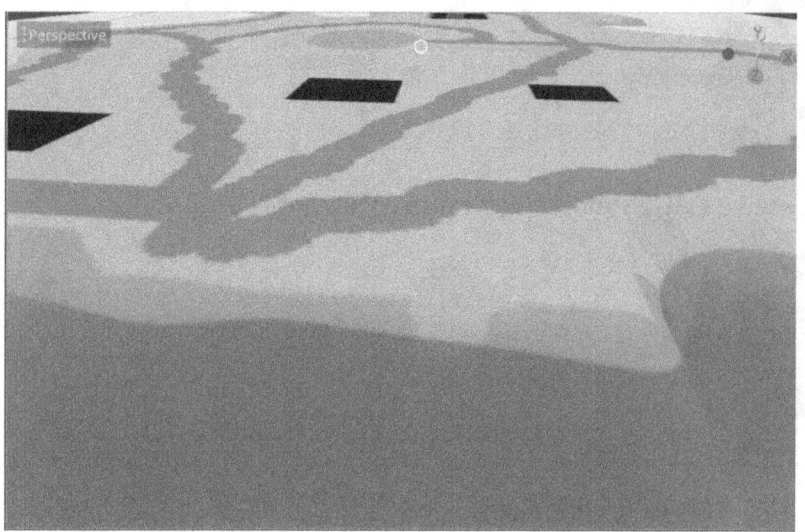

PAINTING THE ISLAND WITH REALISTIC TEXTURES

At this point, the water has been added. This being said, while the original design is great, it would be good to be able to paint the terrain using additional textures or to even erase some of the green circles or the other textures included in the outline. Thankfully, Godot includes a **Texture Paint** tool that makes it possible to literarily paint on the terrain using a wide range of textures. For the **Texture Paint** tool, we avail of a wide range of brushes and settings (e.g., opacity). So let's jazz-up the look of the island and add some textures to it:

- Import the textures called **grass.jpg** and **sandy_color.png** from the resource pack to your project.

- Select the node **HTerrain** in the **Scene Tree** view.

- Select the **Texture Paint** tool from the top toolbar.

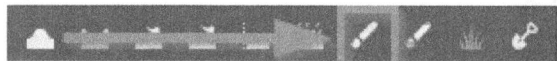

Again, we will need to add a specific texture to this paint brush.

- Using the tab located at the bottom of the window, click on the **Edit** button.

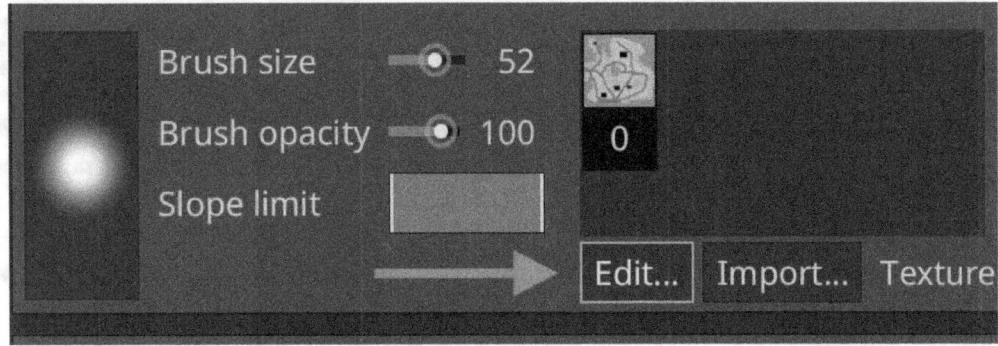

- Then click on the + button located in the left panel to create a new texture.

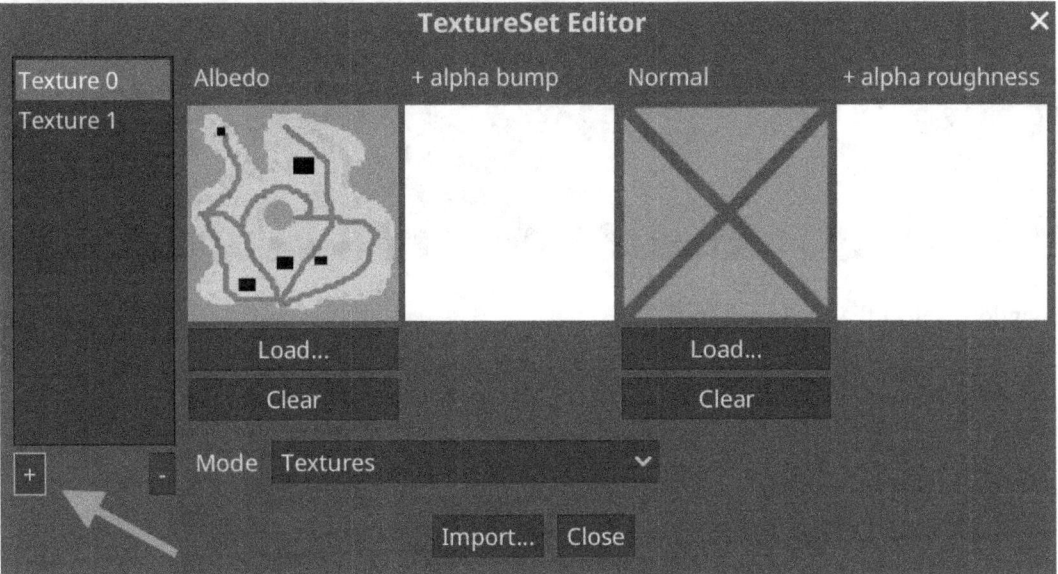

- This will create a new texture called **Texture 1**.

- Click on this texture in the left panel and then click on the button labelled **Load**.

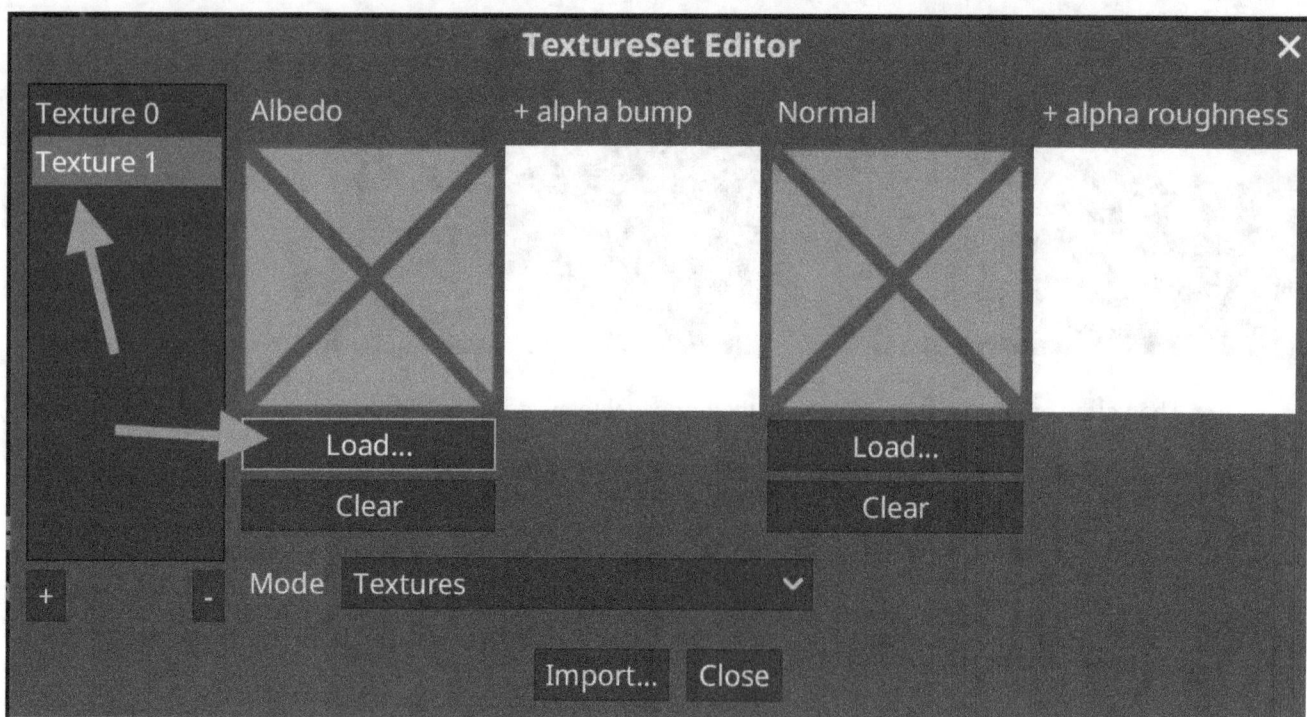

- In the new window, select the file **grass.jpg**.

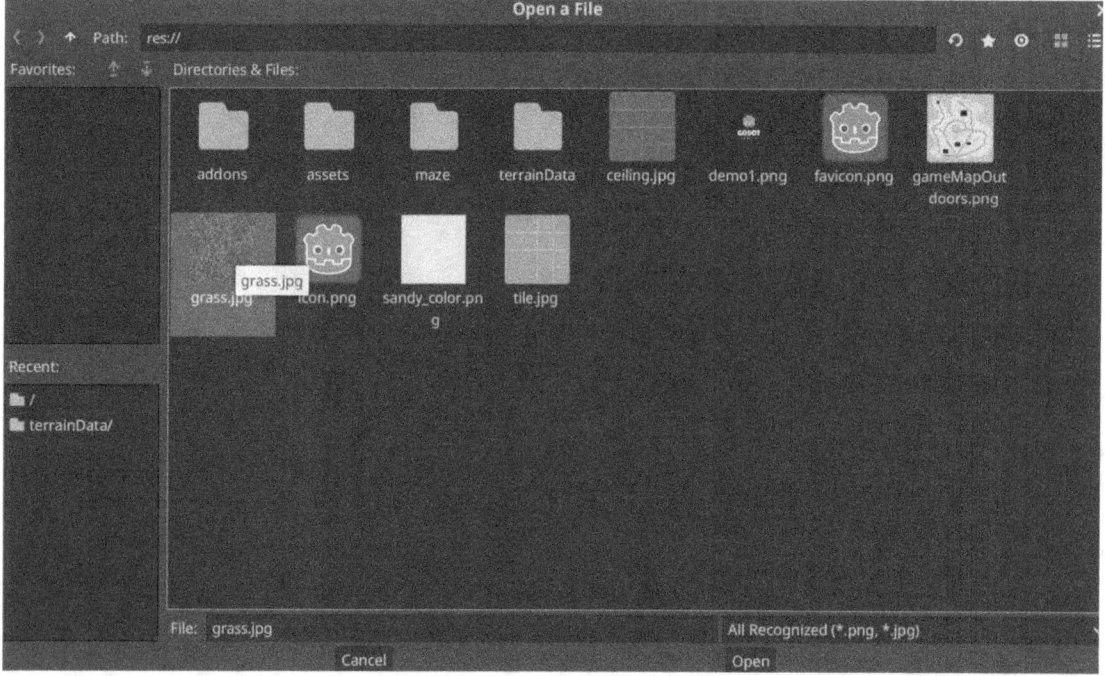

- Click on the button labelled "**Open**" to choose this texture.

- Click **Close** in the next window.

- Once this is done, you should now see that the texture has been added to the available textures for the terrain.

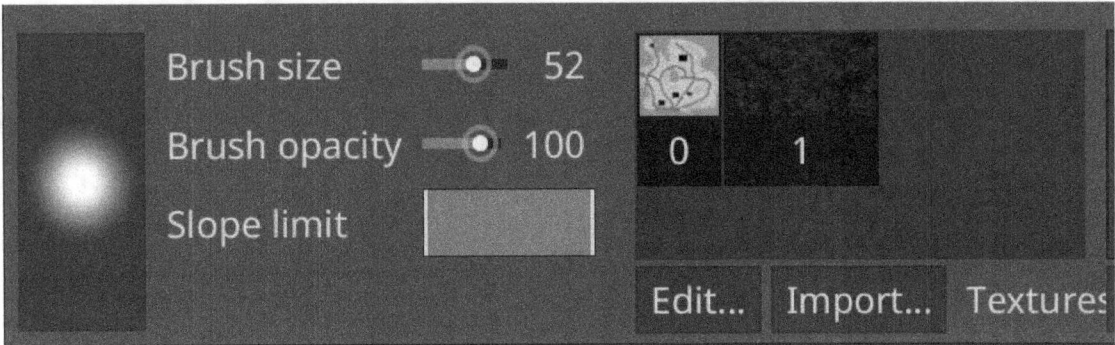

At this stage, you have added a new texture to be used for the terrain.

Reproduce the last steps to add a new texture based on the file **sandy_color.png**.

You should now see three slots, each with the outline of the island, the grass texture, and the sandy texture, respectively in the slots 0,1 and 2.

At this stage, we are ready to paint textures over the island. We could use the second texture to paint some grass areas on the map or delete part of the map by painting a sandy color over; for example:

- Select the sand texture to paint, as illustrated on the next figure.

- Select the **Texture Paint** tool.

- Start to paint over the **Terrain**, for example on the path, and you should notice that it disappears progressively, as illustrated on the next figure.

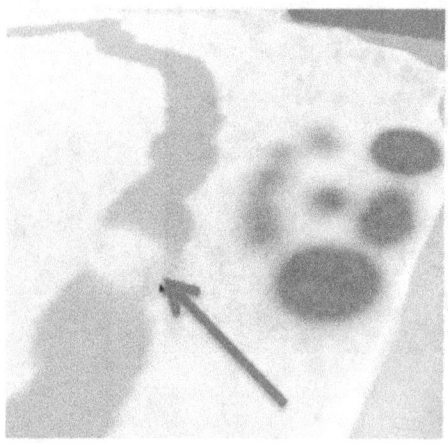

- Using this method, you can delete any of the textures introduced by the map overlay.

- After deleting some of the original path, you can then apply, instead, textures that you have already defined in Godot.

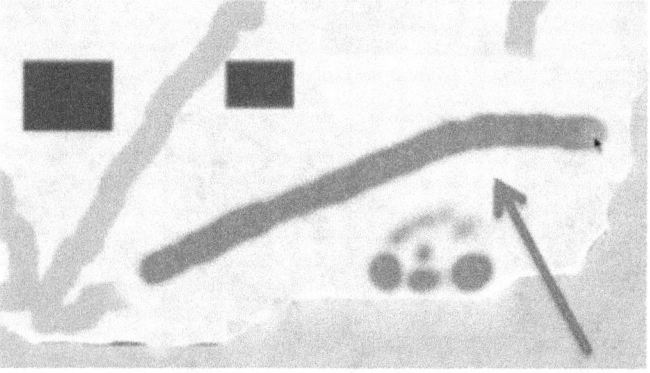

Note that you can also use the Color Paint tool to apply a color (rather than a texture) on the terrain; for this purpose, just select this tool from the top toolbar, and then select the color that you wish to use.

ADDING A LAKE AND A MOUNTAIN

One of the last elements that we need to add is the lake that is located in the middle of the map as well as a mountain. For both elements, we will need to either carve into the terrain (to lower the terrain) or to raise the terrain, and we will be using the tool **Raise/Lower Terrain** for this purpose.

- select the **Terrain** object in the **Hierarchy** view.

- Select the **Lower Height Tool**.

- Locate the lake area on the map and zoom-in.

- Select a brush size of **34** and set its opacity to **100**.

- Drag and drop your mouse (i.e., move) on top of the blue area that defines the lake.

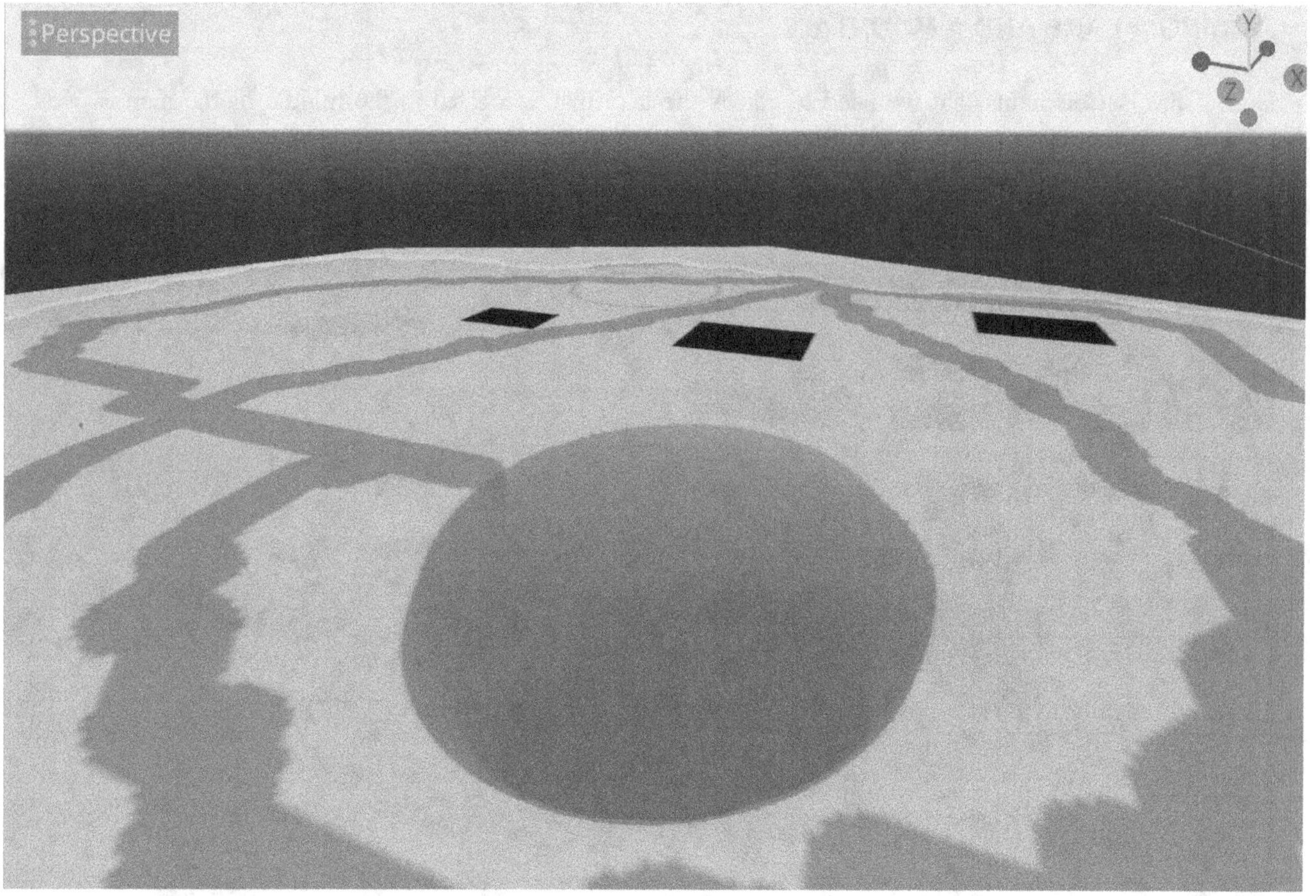

- Using the **Smooth Height** tool, smooth out the boundary of the lake (e.g., you can use a brush size equal to **16**).

Once this is done, we will now create a simple hill using **Raise Height** tool. This hill will be close to the lake in the area highlighted on the next figure.

Once this is done:

- select the **Raise Height** tool.

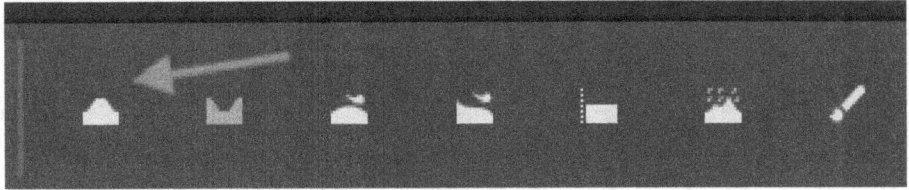

- Select a brush size of **31** and set the opacity to **80**.

- Drag and drop the mouse to the right of the blue area, highlighted by the two red arrows in the previous figure.

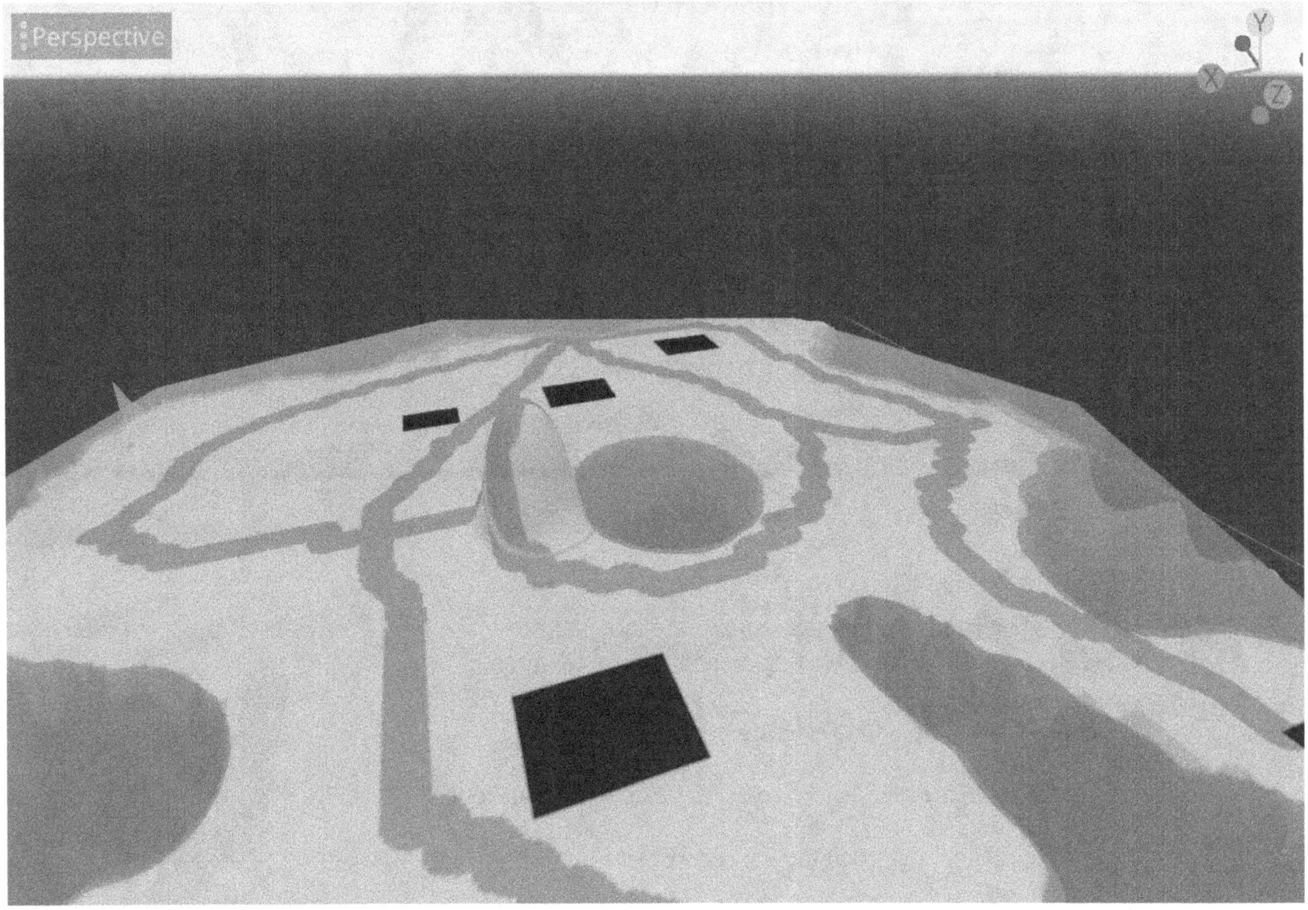

After these modifications, you can pan your view to check that you have managed to raise the ground properly, and it should look as follows (although this could take many iterations, so it's perfectly ok if it does not look exactly like the next image).

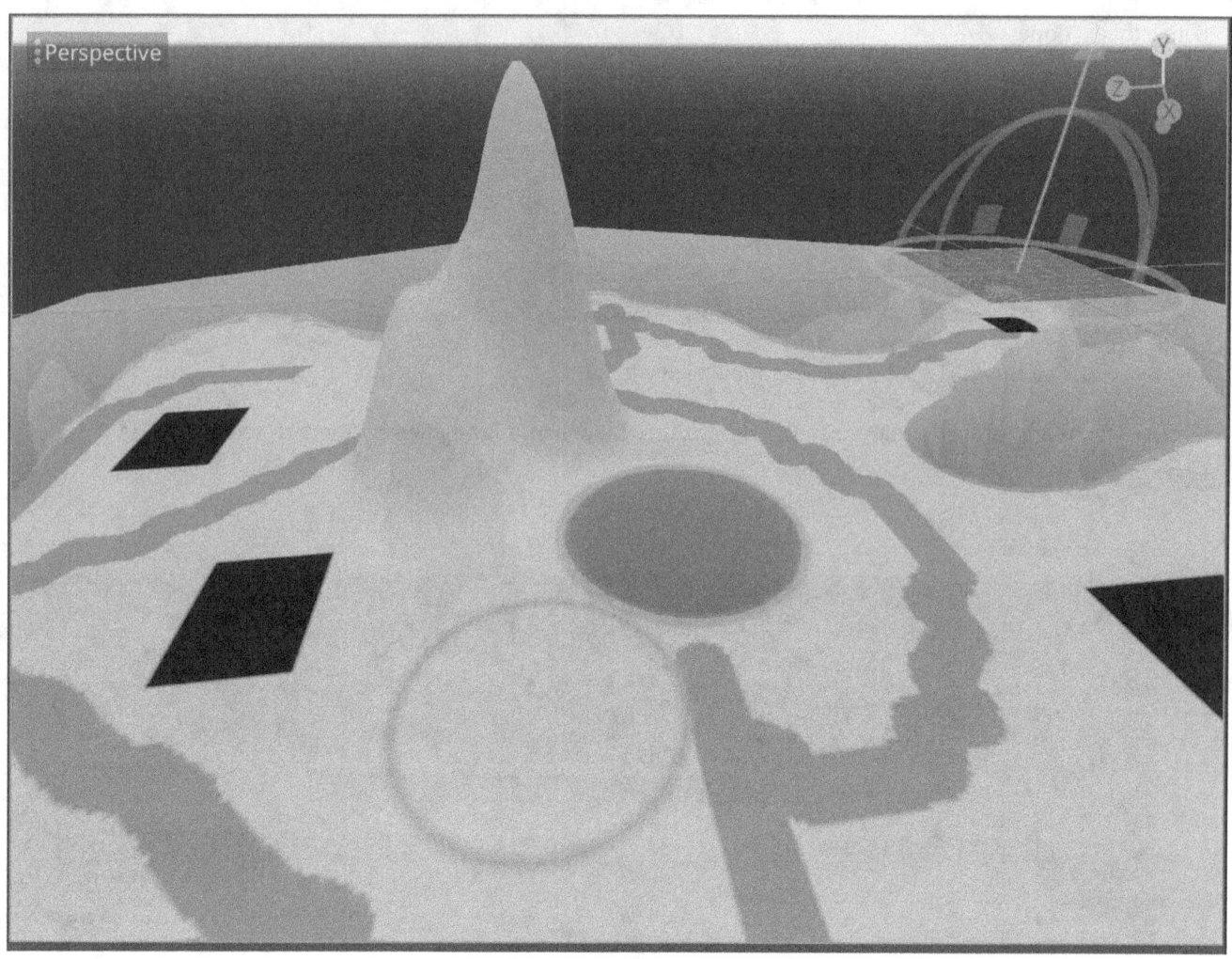

Viewing the hill from above

At this stage, we just need to apply a texture to the mountain to make it look more realistic. As for the ground, we will be using the paint tool after selecting an appropriate texture:

- Select the node labeled **HTerrain**

- Using the toolbar located atop, select the **Texture Paint** tool.

- Select the second texture in the list (i.e., **grass**).

- Use the following settings: **brush size= 14, Opacity = 26**.

- You can now paint the hill. You can either keep the default view in the **Scene** view or switch to a top-down view by clicking on the **y-axis** of the **gizmo**.

- To paint the edges of the mountain, you can use different settings for the brush (e.g., **Opacity = 64**).

- Once you have finished painting the hill, it should look like the one illustrated on the next figure.

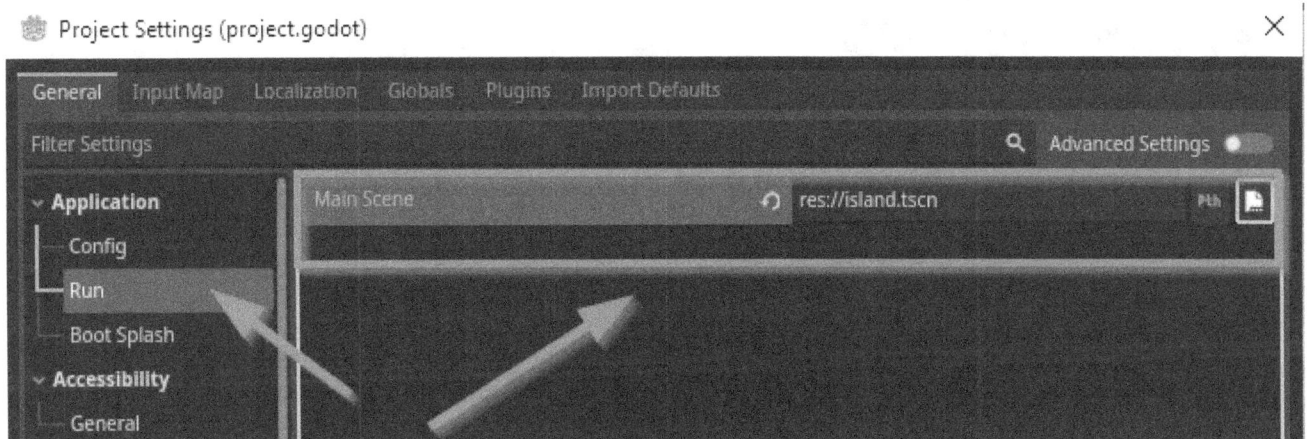

The hill viewed from above

Before we can preview our scene, create a new **Camera3D** node, and sets its Position and rotation to **(220, 40, 220)** and (0, **110, 0)** respectively.

Before you can preview the scene, you will need to modify the **Project Settings**, so that the current scene is now the default one to be played.

You can now either preview the scene using the preview mode for the camera or play the scene (**CTRL + R;** this is to play the scene; you can also press the corresponding button in the top-right corner - the fourth from the left).

Of course, the hill that you have created may look slightly different, and that is perfectly ok.

Note that you can always undo any of your design using *CTRL + Z* or by lowering the areas that you have previously raised.

You can also add a First-Person controller to the scene:

- Delete the node **Camera3D**.

- Drag and drop the item **player.tscn** from the folder **addons | godot4.3_fps_character-controller| Player** (the same controller that you used in the maze scene).

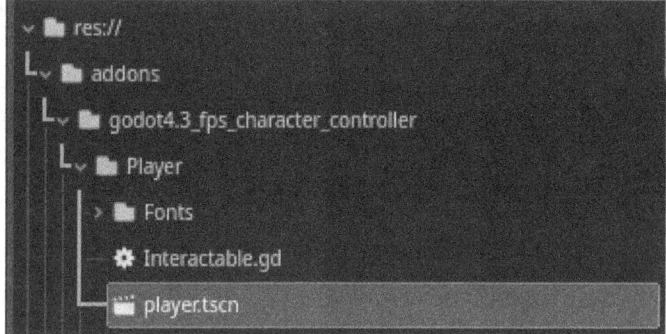

- Make sure it's above the terrain, and play the scene; you should be able to navigate the island, as per the next figure.

ADDING BUILDINGS TO THE ISLAND

We have, at this stage, added all the necessary elements to our island, based on our outline, except from the buildings. These can be created very easily using the same techniques covered in the previous chapters, as you will need to:

- Create new boxes.

- Place and resize these boxes so that they cover the black areas on the outline.

- Scale these boxes on the **y-axis**, using a height of your choice (for example **40**).

Finally, we can add a texture to the buildings. As for previously, you can import a texture, from the resources previously downloaded, called **buildings.jpg**, and then create a new texture for the buildings based on this image (as we have done previously for other objects). You can then modify the tiling for this texture to **(1, 5)** by accessing its corresponding material. This being said, you can use any texture of your choice, including the texture that you have already applied to the tiles for the indoor environment.

- While we have only created the buildings for the first island, you can easily duplicate them twice and position the duplicates on the two additional islands. After adding the buildings, you can play the scene and check how each of them looks like.

LEVEL ROUNDUP

Summary

In this chapter, we have become more comfortable with the creation of indoor and outdoor environments and we learned how to use Godot and the **Asset Library** to create a realistic island. We delved into the different tools available in Godot to create, transform, and texture basic shapes. Well, from finding your way around Godot to creating a realistic island, you can see that you have already made some considerable progress since the start of the book. You have managed to combine your skills, yet with no programming knowledge, to create a truly realistic and interactive environment.

Quiz

It is now time to test your knowledge. state whether the following questions are TRUE or FALSE; the solutions are on the next page.

1. The **AssetLib** window makes it possible to download assets and plugins for Godot.

2. Once a library has been downloaded it needs to be installed.

3. The **Heightmap** terrain library makes it possible to create terrains in Godot.

4. The **Heightmap** doesn't need to be activated before it can be used in Godot.

5. Before using the **Heightmap** library a data folder needs to be created.

6. Only one texture can be applied to a Height Map created with the **Heightmap** library.

7. The **Heightmap** terrain library makes it possible to raise or lower part of a terrain.

8. It is possible to create a terrain with hills and valleys from a simple box object.

9. A camera can't be the child of another object.

10. Its possible to create building from simple boxes.

Solutions to the Quiz

1. TRUE.

2. TRUE.

3. TRUE.

4. FALSE.

5. TRUE.

6. FALSE.

7. TRUE.

8. FALSE.

9. FALSE.

10. TRUE.

Checklist

If you can do the following, then you are ready to go to the next chapter:

- Create a terrain.

- Raise and lower parts of the terrain.

- Add textures to the terrain.

- Add (and track with a camera) a car that includes an embedded camera.

Challenge 1

For this challenge, you will need to create a new outdoor environment, based on a new template as follows:

- Import the texture **gameMapOutline2.png** from the folders that you have downloaded from the companion site.

- Create a new scene.

- Apply the same techniques as before to recreate the island.

- Add a car.

Challenge 2

For this challenge, you will need to create your own outline, using the image manipulation tool of your choice, and then apply it to create a new island of your own design!

You could proceed as follows:

- Create a new image with a size of 500 pixels by 500 pixels.

- Set the background to white.

- Create the outline of the island using a brush of size 1.

- Add green, blue, or brown areas to identify the position of trees, water, or paths.

- Save your image in the **jpg** or **png** format.

- Import this image into Godot.

- Create a new scene.

- Use this new template to create your new outdoor scene.

CHAPTER 6: FREQUENTLY ASKED QUESTIONS

This chapter provides answers to the most frequently asked questions about the features that we have covered in this book.

NAVIGATION

How do I navigate through my scene?

Import and install the libraries **3DCar with SettingsPanel** or **Simple First Person Controller**.

After importing my Simple First Person Controller I still can't move around the scene.

Make sure that you have configured the **Input** map so that the arrow keys are linked to the proper keywords (e.g., **player_forwards**).

TRANSFORMATIONS AND ASSETS

How do I import assets in my scene?

Import the asset (e.g., texture, image or sound) by dragging and dropping this asset inside the **FileSystem** dock in Godot.

How can I transform objects?

You can select the object and then either use the key shortcuts (i.e., W, E, R, and T) or modify the object's transform properties in the **Inspector** window.

CREATING, ORGANISING AND SEARCHING FOR OBJECTS AND ASSETS

How do I create an object?

Select the node **Node3D Node**, and press **CTRL + A** (or right-click).

How do I add a texture?

Click on the downward facing arrow to the right of the attribute called **Material** for the object. You can then, in the new contextual menu, select the option called **New Node3DMaterial**.

How do I group objects?

Create an empty object (parent) and drag-and-drop the objects to be grouped on the parent.

How do I look for objects in my project?

Use the project search window and search by name.

If I import an asset in my project, can I access it from any scene within this project?

Yes, and that's a very interesting feature that will save some space on your hard drive.

CHAPTER 7: THANK YOU

I would like to thank you for completing this book. I trust that you are now comfortable with Godot and that you can create interactive 3D environments.

This book is the first in a series of four books on Godot, and while you have learned a lot in this book, you will need to learn more to be able to master Godot, create a wide range of games and get to learn GDScript.

While a sequel to this book is in the pipeline, you can always email me and let me know if you would like to see a sequel to this book and what features you'd like to learn (e.g., GD Script).

Before you do so, leave an honest review on the e-book store of your choice.

So that the book can be constantly improved, I would really appreciate your feedback and hear what you have to say. So, leave me a helpful review letting me know what you thought of the book and also send me an email (**learntocreategames@gmail.com**) with any suggestion you may have. I read and reply to every email.

Thanks so much!!

- Pat